Open Education

DISRUPTIONS

Disruptions is a series that interrogates and analyses disruptions within and across such fields and disciplines as culture and society, media and technology, literature and philosophy, aesthetics and politics.

Series Editor

Paul Bowman, Reader, Cardiff School of Journalism, Media and Cultural Studies, Cardiff University, UK

Editorial Review Board

Bearing Society in Mind: Theories and Politics of the Social Formation, Samuel A. Chambers

Open Education: A Study in Disruption, Pauline van Mourik Broekman, Gary Hall, Ted Byfield, Shaun Hides and Simon Worthington

What Lies Between: Void Aesthetics and Postwar Politics, Matt Tierney (forthcoming)

Living Screens: Reading Melodrama in Contemporary Film and Television, Monique Rooney (forthcoming)

Word: Divine, Dissonant and Digital, Mariam Motamedi Fraser (forthcoming)

Martial Arts Studies, Paul Bowman (forthcoming)

Open Education

A Study in Disruption

Pauline van Mourik Broekman, Gary Hall,
Ted Byfield, Shaun Hides, and Simon Worthington

ROWMAN &
LITTLEFIELD
——INTERNATIONAL

London • New York

Published by Rowman & Littlefield International, Ltd.
16 Carlisle Street, London, W1D 3BT
www.rowmaninternational.com

Rowman & Littlefield International, Ltd. is an affiliate of
Rowman & Littlefield
4501 Forbes Boulevard, Suite 200, Lanham, Maryland 20706, USA
With additional offices in Boulder, New York, Toronto (Canada),
    and Plymouth (UK)
www.rowman.com

British Library Cataloguing in Publication Data
A catalogue record for this book is available from the British Library

ISBN: HB 978-1-78348-208-5
    PB 978-1-78348-209-2

Library of Congress Cataloging-in-Publication Data Available
        978-1-78348-208-5 (cloth : alk. paper)
        978-1-78348-209-2 (pbk. : alk. paper)
        978-1-78348-210-8 (electronic)

∞™ The paper used in this publication meets the minimum requirements of
American National Standard for Information Sciences—Permanence of Paper for
Printed Library Materials, ANSI/NISO Z39.48-1992.

Printed in the United States of America

Contents

Preface

Many have observed that all around the world, the current protests are driven by debt-ridden students and graduates without a future. The precarious middle class, in short ('lost a job, found an occupation'). At the same time, the numbers tell us that the worst hit are the working and marginalised classes, mostly across the colour line. The next big movements could easily look quite different. In all likelihood we are headed towards an even more extensive social crisis.

I think in this context and at this moment there is a potential role for what you could call the intelligentsia (or Gramsci's organic intellectuals) to seize the cultural and technical resources of the university system, while bending both the rules of discourse and the order of bodies, actively looking for different participants and more practical-political ideas. The point is to find a cross-class, multiracial and multigender way of dealing with social complexity—because that has been the great claim of neoliberalism so far, and there's no way around it, we have to do it better than them.

—Brian Holmes[1]

This book has been written as part of an ongoing collaboration between Mute Publishing and the Media Department at Coventry School of Art and Design. It has emerged from our shared interest in digital culture, theory, politics, and the ability of new forms of networked technologies, open access digital publishing, collaborative web tools, and sociable spaces to both help enhance and disrupt educational activity. In the background to this collaboration lies the research of Coventry University's Centre for Disruptive Media, with its key theme of Open Media,[2] and Mute Publishing's exploration of the relationships between technology, culture, and society since its founding in 1994—expressed in editorial work, via *Mute* magazine, as well as software and infrastructures development, via the digital services agency OpenMute.[3]

Our exchange began with an interrogation of the potential role of hybrid publishing tools and techniques in the Media Department's provision of course materials. In spring 2012 Coventry decided to structure the relationship more actively so as to draw out a stronger strategic direction for the collaboration. It drew up a commission for Mute Publishing to work with the department's Open Media Group and its Centre for Disruptive Media to produce a multi-part project. This was to consist of:

- An open access, collaborative research wiki hosting a contemporary analysis of the global phenomenon of Open Education (OpenCourseWare, MOOCs, TED, Wikiversity, aaaaarg, et al.). The analysis was intended to situate, contextualise, and orient Coventry University's own activity in this area and be made available on an open access, 'liquid' basis enabling it to be edited, changed, updated, reversioned, and used to produce derivative works.
- A book, also engaging with the burgeoning phenomenon of Open Education, co-authored by Coventry's Open Media Group, the co-directors of Mute Publishing, and their long-time collaborator, the educator and author Ted Byfield.

This book, designed as a critical and creative experiment with collaborative, processual modes of writing, and concise (hence the occasional use of bullet points), medium-length forms of shared attention, is one of the outcomes of that more active relationship. Embarking on the initial stages of research for this book, it quickly became clear that the subject of Open Education was not only vast, but also experiencing an explosion of activity and disruptive change that would be difficult to capture in a relatively small-scale project such as ours. We concluded that attempts at a comprehensive overview could detract from our main objective of developing a strategic philosophy with regard to

Open Education. Taking into account the approaches of our respective organisations, we agreed that our guiding priorities and assumptions throughout the book should be as follows:

- We use the generic 'Open Education' as our central term of reference. This designates an activity *and* practice, and can on that basis be distinguished from other existing monikers, like 'Open Educational Resources' (OER), which we will only use to describe educational materials made available on an open basis. Since, in practice, 'OER' tends to be reflective of a distinct history of technical, legal, and/or funding frameworks (some of the most significant of which will reappear later in this book: for example, the William and Flora Hewlett Foundation), it is more geographically and politically determined than we would like our central term to be. Our perspective remains a British one, even if North American frameworks and initiatives dominate debate in the Open Education field and so inevitably provide our initial guide.[4]
- We prioritise the activities of Higher Education Institutions (HEIs), but, to reflect the dramatically changing landscape of Open Education and define it as broadly as possible, consider these in tandem with grassroots and entrepreneurial initiatives.
- Mirroring most Open Education (OE) discourses, we have no typical student or 'user' in mind: students can participate in OE within and without conventional HEIs, and, while they are certainly due their own, dedicated critical treatment, we reflect the widespread movement internationally towards models of 'lifelong learning' (that is, we assume a modularity for the educational experience, with ad-hoc decisions over progression based on the contingencies of individual lives).
- In line with this, we insist on an awareness of the significant role played by so-called piracy, and 'pirated' educational materials, and resist condemnation of their use.
- We recommend a proactive engagement with technical and legal issues, even if these are not always our central focus in this book.
- We hold higher education to be a site where the interests of diverse constituencies come together yet exist in a state of tension and conflict—and are often demonstrably incompatible.

The last assumption should be regarded as governing all others. It contends that, in educational environments, things are often intertwined to a degree that makes discrete analyses and the establishment of fixed and firm boundaries difficult, if not impossible. Moreover, because the field is suffused with *aspirations* and necessarily depends on *cooperation*, it lends itself to speculative discourses that draw attention from what *is* to what *could be*. In our view, this means one effective way to understand HEIs is as sites of contestation between divergent constituencies whose needs are often incommensurate and operating on disparate timescales.

The following table, though reductive, indicates how disparate the respective worlds of these constituencies can be. The 'dilemma' column suggests how varied the challenges each 'group' faces are and, in particular, how efforts to resolve them play out in time understood in different ways—day to day, annual, occasional (for example, due to 'opportunities' or political initiatives), life/career-planning, institutional, and so on.

This type of model is of course extremely problematic. Still, its virtue is to emphasise the complex, multi-perspectival field in which Open Education takes place: not as a singular ideal for the public good, but rather as an assemblage of aspects and tendencies that may seem more or less relevant and appealing (or not) to the various actors and constituencies to whom it is presented as, among other things, a legal/technical problem, an opportunity to cut or divert expenditure, a font of no-charge educational materials, and so forth.

For example, the peer/mentor relations that are a central feature of education for many students are not typically associated with the value of standardisation that is so important to administrators and government functionaries. Yet with the rise of the 'BYOD' (Bring Your Own Device) approach garnering attention in IT circles, the 'friction' associated with technical problem solving involving different devices and platforms is a widely noted basis for peer learning. Many people now take it for granted that web discussion boards and similar resources are a go-to source for solving technical problems. However, these discussions are rarely cited as a de facto example of the values of Open Education.

Indeed, institutional adoption of Open Education approaches necessarily involves complex policy negotiations between constituencies,

Higher Education Constituencies and Dilemmas They Face

Constituency	Dilemma	Focus	Goals
at-large population	study vs. work	cost, access, career/calling	advance, sociability, meeting obligations
students	exploration vs. focus	individual, aspirational, changing time frames	pragmatism, inspiration, peer/ mentor relations
faculty	progress vs. position	inquiry, pluralism, tradeoffs	research, dissemination, teaching
administrators/ ops	expansion vs. maintenance	institutional, maintenance, logistics	standardization, integration, adoption
govt/ supervisory	innovation vs. status quo	hierarchy, process, public perceptions	standardization, compliance, performance
civil society	confrontation vs. pragmatism	ideals, access, alliances	policy, implementation, funding
vendors	short vs. long term	commercial, systematic, strategic	profit, growth, lock-in, standardization

and in these negotiations the conceptual model of education that is presented—as a site of contention between different actors with conflicting interests—can become somewhat fixed. Thus, for example, rights-holders often use policy processes as an opportunity to lock in revenue streams and establish the broadest possible understandings of what their rights might entail. The problem, of course, is that key constituencies—notably students, but also faculty—are rarely if ever represented as such in policy-making processes.

NOTES

1. Brian Holmes, 'A Movement Without Demands?', <nettime-l> mailing list, January 5, 2011, http://www.nettime.org/Lists-Archives/nettime-l-1201/msg00020.html.

2. The Centre for Disruptive Media has evolved out of a number of historical projects, the shared aim of many of which is to develop a proactive stance on open access and Open Education. These projects include but are not limited to: a formal Open Media policy and Open Access (OA) mandate for the Media Department at Coventry School of Art and Design (the third Green OA Mandate for a Humanities Department in the World, the first nationally, the U.K.'s twenty-fourth Green OA Mandate, and the planet's ninety-second); four 'open' courses, the longest running of which—PICBOD (for Picturing the Body)—dates back to 2009; further Open Access and Open Media–related initiatives (i.e., *Culture Machine*, Open Humanities Press, Liquid Theory TV, the *Living Books about Life* series); and a range of sister initiatives within Coventry University, engaging with creative archiving and digitisation in culture, as well as new forms of learning (the Siobhan Davies Archive, D-TRACES, Shakespeare Byte-Size, the Disruptive Media Learning Lab, and so on). More information can be found at http://disruptivemedia.org.uk/.

3. Mute Publishing's editorial archive is available at http://www.metamute.org; the organisation's software development and digital strategy work is catalogued at http://www.metamute.org/services. Since 2012, these two strands of activity have also been shaped by a two-year collaboration with the University of Lüneburg, Leuphana, conducted via the editorial-curatorial project, the Post-Media Lab, and software development project, the Hybrid Publishing Consortium (see http://www.postmedialab.org and http://hybridpublishing.org/consortium/). Mute magazine has, since the ending of the Post-Media Lab project in Spring 2014, been run collectively by its editorial board and project manager, an arrangement which is intended to replace publication by Mute Publishing. For more on the magazine's history, see Nick Thoburn,

'*Ceci n'est pas un magazine*: The Politics of Hybrid Media in *Mute* Magazine', *New Media and Society*, December 5, 2011, http://nms.sagepub.com/content/early/2011/12/05/1461444811427532.full.pdf+html; and Julian Stallabrass, 'Digital Partisans: *Mute* and the Cultural Politics of the Net', *New Left Review*, 2012, http://newleftreview.org/II/74/julian-stallabrass-digital-partisans.

4. In this respect, we agreed it would not be necessary to include exact statistics on the capitalisation, uptake, turnover or media content of each Open Education player in the comparator exercises we intended to perform (see Section 5, 'Open Education Typologies'), nor to detail significant contextual subjects—for example, intellectual property rights, human rights, global/national governance, and state regulation—unless they bore direct and immediate relevance to our argument.

1

❖ ❖

The University in the
Twenty-First Century

There are at least two reasons it is important to experiment, critically and creatively, with the institution of the university at this
particular moment in its history. In the chapter 'The Rise of the Global
University' in his 2009 book, *Nice Work If You Can Get It*, Andrew
Ross predicts that it is only a matter of time before we see the begin-
nings of a global university on the 'model of the global corporation'
such as News Corporation, Time Warner, Coca-Cola, Elsevier, and
Pearson.[1] He proceeds to present a somewhat gloomy vision of the future for universities if, in their drive to be ever more business-like and
profit-orientated, they continue to follow the corporate model:

> In this labor-intensive industry (the majority of education costs go to
> teaching labor), the instructional budget is where an employer will seek
> to minimize costs first, usually by introducing distance learning or by
> hiring offshore instructors at large salary discounts. Expatriate employ-
> ees—assigned to set up an offshore facility, train locals, and provide cred-
> ibility for the brand—will be a fiscal liability to be offloaded at the first
> opportunity. If the satellite campus is located in the same industrial park
> as *Fortune* 500 firms, then it will almost certainly be invited to produce
> customized research for these companies, again at discount prices. It will
> only be a matter of time before an administrator decides that it will be
> cost-effective to move some domestic research operations to the overseas
> branch to save money.

As far as the domestic record goes, higher education institutions have followed much the same trail as subcontracting in industry—first, the outsourcing of all non-academic campus personnel, then the casualization of routine instruction, followed by the creation of a permatemps class on short-term contracts, and the preservation of an ever-smaller core of tenure-track full-timers, crucial to the brand prestige of the collegiate name. Downward salary pressure and eroded job security are the inevitable upshot.[2]

As Ross's account of the U.S. domestic situation suggests, we should take care not to console ourselves too quickly with the thought that such globalised corporate scenarios belong to an as yet still distant *future*. In fact just one year after the publication of *Nice Work If You Can Get It*, an article in the U.S. *Chronicle of Higher Education* detailed how the director of business law and ethics studies at the University of Houston was outsourcing the grading of undergraduate papers to Virtual-TA, a service of a company called EduMetry Inc., whose employees are mostly in Asia:

> The goal of the service is to relieve professors and teaching assistants of a traditional and sometimes tiresome task—and even, the company says, to do it better than TA's [teaching assistants] can. The graders working for EduMetry, based in a Virginia suburb of Washington, are concentrated in India, Singapore, and Malaysia, along with some in the United States and elsewhere. They do their work online and communicate with professors via e-mail. . . . The company argues that professors freed from grading papers can spend more time teaching and doing research.[3]

Even closer to home, the United Kingdom's University of Warwick and Australia's Monash University announced in February 2012 that they had formed a partnership aimed at enabling both institutions to compete in the 'globalised higher education market'. Ed Byrne, Monash's vice chancellor and former director of private healthcare firm Bupa, was quoted in *Times Higher Education* as saying that, thanks to globalisation and technological change, higher education 'is really going to become a global marketplace', a process which will 'alter the traditional university model'. The same article has Byrne echoing an airline analogy used by his Warwick counterpart Nigel Thrift to emphasise the potential of such global university partnerships: 'in the Star Alliance that includes Lufthansa and United Airlines, independent brands had realised that "to cover the globe" they "needed to come together to form a different type of partnership"'. Hence the reason the 'two vice-chancellors believe that global "university systems" will be needed to respond to future demands in education and research'.[4]

Yet if we are highly critical of the way universities today, in their drive to be ever more business-like and profit-orientated, *are* closely following the corporate model, complete with distance learning, outsourcing, off-shoring, global 'university systems', and all, and at the same time have no desire to return to the paternalistic and class-bound ideas that previously dominated the university, replete with all the hierarchies and exclusions around differences of class, race, gender, ethnicity, and so forth they imply, then what—to echo the title of Cardinal Newman's book from the nineteenth century—is *our* idea of the university?[5] Or as Stefan Collini has recently put it when offering his own (albeit ultimately rather conservative) response to this question, *What Are Universities For?*[6] We shall return to these queries throughout the argument that follows.

A second and related reason for embarking on an experimental project around the institution of the university at this particular moment in time concerns the central role higher education plays in twenty-first-century global capitalism's 'knowledge economy'. In the past, 'the factory was a paradigmatic site of struggle between workers and capitalists'. However, it has been argued that in today's cognitive capitalism it is the university that is a 'key space of conflict, where the ownership of knowledge, the reproduction of the labour force, and the creation of social and cultural stratifications are all at stake. The university, in other words, is not just another institution subject to sovereign and governmental controls, but a crucial site in which wider social struggles are won and lost'[7]—and all the more so post-2008, a point in time which signals the beginning of the so-called global financial crisis and the age of 'austerity'. The importance of the university as a site of struggle may explain why the police and the British state are reacting to student and staff protests against the future direction of higher education with such extreme force. In December 2010, many of those demonstrating outside parliament in London against the introduction of university tuition fees found themselves met with a surprisingly violent response on the part of the police. This involved being kettled, struck with batons, and charged with horses. Since then a number of activists have been given harsh prison sentences. They include Charlie Gilmour, a student at Cambridge, who was sentenced to twelve months for, among other things, swinging from a union flag on the Cenotaph war memorial in London's Whitehall; Edward Woollard, a schoolboy, given two years and eight months for throwing a fire extinguisher from the roof of Conservative Party headquarters in November 2010; and Francis Fernie, who had just completed his A-levels at the time of a March 2011 protest against the austerity cuts. He was sentenced to twelve months for throwing the sticks from two placards outside the upmarket department store Fortnum & Mason. Meanwhile, Alfie Meadows, a university student who was struck on the head with a police baton during the 2010 protests and left with bleeding on the brain, had to face a long, drawn-out trial before finally being found not guilty of violent disorder in March 2013.

Protests are continuing nevertheless. From October 2013 onwards a number of university occupations have taken place with a view to opposing privatisation, including the outsourcing of services and the selling off of the student debt created by the introduction of tuition fees. On December 4, police evicted protesters from an occupation at the University of London, with many of the latter again alleging police brutality. Forty-one students were subsequently arrested. Over the same period two students at the University of Birmingham were asked to pay tens of thousands in court costs for their role in an occupation, while five students were suspended from the University of Sussex for similar actions.

In the light of the above events, some political analysts have gone so far as to claim that, if anywhere, political revolt today is most likely to come from the middle classes, in part due to the increasing cost of the education they need to sustain their position in a society where, according to the U.K. Office of National Statistics, 40 per cent of the national wealth is owned by just 10 per cent of the population, and wages for low- to middle-income families are predicted to be the same in 2020 as they were in 2000.[8] This is certainly one of the explanations given for the most recent wave of protests. The December 4 occupation at the University of London, for example, had its basis in the '3 Cosas' campaign in support of outsourced service staff at London universities—many of them workers from Latin America—and their demands for equal rights with other university workers, including sick pay, holiday pay and pensions.[9] So students and lower-level members of the teaching body are clearly fighting not just for themselves and their own interests: they realize they have more in common with these service workers than with the highly paid vice chancellors who are busy turning their institutions into businesses. (The highest paid vice chancellor in the United Kingdom is the Open University's Martin Bean, who in the academic year up to August 2013 had a salary of £407,000—possibly because he was recruited from Microsoft. But others are not far behind. They include the LSE's Craig Calhoun, who received £466,000—although reportedly £88,000 of that was to cover his relocation expenses from the United States.)[10] The protesters are also conscious that, far from a university education being a route to social mobility and financial security as it might once have been, many of today's undergraduates will have debts of around £50,000 when they graduate, and that they themselves are likely to become low-waged precarious workers—if they can get a job at all.

Interestingly, while further *middle-class* protests have taken place in Brazil in 2013 and in Thailand in 2014, the U.K. Ministry of Defence was referring to the role of what it called 'The Middle Class Proletariat' as far back as 2007:

> The Middle Class Proletariat—The middle classes could become a revolutionary class, taking the role envisaged for the proletariat by Marx. The globalization of labour markets and reducing levels of national welfare provision and employment could reduce peoples' attachment to particular states. The growing gap between themselves and a small number of highly visible super-rich individuals might fuel disillusion with meritocracy, while the growing urban under-classes are likely to pose an increasing threat to social order and stability, as the burden of acquired debt and the failure of pension provision begins to bite. Faced by these twin challenges, the world's middle-classes might unite, using access to knowledge, resources and skills to shape transnational processes in their own class interest.[11]

From this perspective, the university today does indeed emerge as a key site of political struggle: not just in the United Kingdom at UCL, Birmingham, Sussex, Middlesex, Leeds, Westminster, SOAS, and Goldsmiths, but also internationally, with protests and occupations having taken place in recent years in the United States, Canada,

Germany, Austria, Italy, Greece, Puerto Rico, Argentina, and Chile.[12] This is no doubt one reason why so many experiments involving attempts to rethink the university have emerged over this period, with the list of such projects including the Occupy University (and its London variant, Tent City University), The Really Free School, Chicago Mess Hall, The Public School, Worker's Punk University, Free Slow University of Warsaw, and the University for Strategic Optimism.[13] The political ideologies of these projects are many and varied, but as Dougald Hine—himself a co-founder of a grassroots platform turned dotcom, School of Everything—writes:

> There's something important coming together around networked technologies and new sociable collaboration spaces, that's beginning to feel plausible as an alternative home for the spirit of the university. And it's happening just as long-term strains within existing institutions, together with the acute effects of economic crisis, are prompting many people to look for such an alternative.
>
> If a major disruption of our existing institutional forms is under way, then this is also a good time for a deeper enquiry into the promise at the heart of the university, the social good for which it has provided a home, and the ways in which this is (or isn't) made available to people through both existing institutions and emerging alternatives.[14]

Given our interest in the ability of new forms of networked technologies, open access digital publishing, collaborative web tools, and sociable spaces to help enhance and disrupt educational activity, the 'free', self-organised learning communities, or 'universities', that have emerged in recent years, not least with the student and anti-austerity protests and global Occupy movement, have undoubtedly served as one of the motivating impulses behind the production of this book. Despite our recognition of the importance of these wider political events and movements, however, we have taken the decision not to comment substantially on them here. Not because we consider them to be uninteresting or unimportant with regard to thinking about how we might experiment with the institution of the university. Far from it. It is more that, if it is an articulation of these events and movements that is required, then a good deal of interesting work is already available on the subject, including contributions from Alain Badiou, Manuel Castells, Noam Chomsky, and Michael Hardt and Antonio Negri and, in a less celebratory register, from the editorial collective Endnotes.[15] We are also wary of using these recent political occurrences as intellectual capital: as an opportunity to reinforce our *own* position and credentials as an engaged group of collaborators. Is there not a danger that attempts—particularly on the part of those of us who work 'in' the university—to represent, or speak to, these protests and movements (even when we do so in an approving fashion that is critical of other intellectual, societal, and governmental responses) may actually fly in the face of a lot of what they are about? Do slogans such as 'They don't represent us' not point towards a non-representational political practice, one that goes beyond the idea that the politicians of representative democracy support the interests of the 1 per cent rather than those of the people?[16] In addition, it seems to us that political discourses of *urgency* and *crisis* around the student and anti-austerity protests, global Occupy movement, Arab Spring, and so on often risk closing off access to the 'political', and the decision as to what should be written about and responded to most urgently.[17]

Certainly, we support many of the ideas and values behind the creation, 'outside' of the established institutions, of free, autonomous, self-organised universities that anyone can be part of and which, because of their insistence that the whole of mainstream society needs to change, often refuse to make demands of any of its specific (institutional) manifestations. At the same time we would maintain that:

- There is no *outside* to the university in any simple sense, this idea of an outside to the university being itself an academic (that is, a philosophical) idea, even if it is one that has not been theorized rigorously.
- Efforts to occupy a place or space that is autonomous from the traditional university (whether they are physically located outside the institution or not) too often end up unwittingly trapped inside it, in the sense of unconsciously repeating many of its structures and problems. In particular, such efforts tend to take insufficient account of the way many of those involved in establishing such supposedly *autonomous* institutions are themselves the products of, and maintain a relationship with, the traditional university. (After all, if what was reported is true, and some of those who

took part in the 2011 student actions in London were familiar with the writings of Guy Debord and the Situationists, this is at least partly because these texts are taught on many university courses in the arts and humanities.) Moreover, the university is also one of the places where some of those involved in the creation of such autonomous institutions find employment and support from time to time.

- Attacking the 'public' university poses a danger of lending force to neoliberalism's practice of bolstering global corporate institutions while simultaneously undermining nearly all others.
- There is a case to be made for supporting and defending the university as one of the few remaining public spaces where difficult, challenging, and avowedly non-commercial ideas can still be developed, explored, and disseminated (to a certain extent at least). Indeed, as the most recent wave of student protests attests, the university is one of the few places where the imposition of neoliberalism and its emphasis on production, privatisation, and the interests of the market is still being struggled over or even actively resisted.
- Creating autonomous universities 'outside' of the established institutions risks leaving the traditional university itself, along with its emerging role in the global knowledge economy as 'edu factory', in place and unquestioned.

Yet while appreciating any attempt to move beyond the institution is already itself an institutional move, is it possible to take impetus and inspiration from the emergence from within and across activist, artistic, and educational fields of autonomous and self-organised learning communities nonetheless? What if we, too, in our capacity as academics, authors, writers, publishers, critics, thinkers, researchers, and scholars wish to counter the continued imposition of a neoliberal political rationality that may appear dead on its feet but, zombie-like, is still managing to stumble on? Are there ways we can refuse to simply submit critical thought to 'existing political discourses and the formulation of political needs those discourses articulate'—thus 'defusing' what Merleau-Ponty called 'the trap of the event'[18]—and act not so much *for* or *with* the 'remainder of capital', anti-austerity protesters, and 'graduates without a future', but *in terms of* them, as Michel Foucault put it when asked whether he wrote *The Use of Pleasure* and *The Care of the Self* 'for the liberation movement'?[19] Does the struggle against the 'becoming business' of the university not require us, too, to have the courage to experiment with new systems and models for the production, publication, sharing, and discussion of teaching, learning, and research; and thus to open ourselves to transforming radically the material practices and social relations of our institutional labour?[20]

DISRUPTIVE MEDIA

It is with a view to exploring these questions that the Centre for Disruptive Media has been established at Coventry University and this project on the disruptive effect of networked media technologies on educational activity devised and produced (see the preface). The term disruption, in the sense we are using it, has its origins with the economic theory of Karl Marx, according to which capitalist develop-ment occurs as a result of the *creative destruction* of the previous eco-nomic system.[21] The concept of creative destruction was subsequently adapted in the twentieth century by the economist Joseph Schumpeter to refer to the cycle of business innovation, what is now sometimes known as 'Schumpeter's gale'. Disruption has been given a further spin more recently by Clayton Christensen, professor of business administration at Harvard Business School, in the guise of disruptive technology, a concept he uses to develop his theory of the innovator's dilemma. A disruptive technology, for Christensen, is one that facili-tates the production of a new market and a new network of values, and eventually succeeds in disrupting an already established market and value network. An example is provided by mobile telephones. Through their built-in cameras, these phones have disrupted the market for compact analogue and digital cameras, thus leading Kodak, which at one time had 90 per cent of film and 85 per cent of camera sales in the United States, to file for bankruptcy in 2012. Christensen's argument is that 'disruptive technologies typically enable new markets to emerge', and that those organisations 'entering these markets early have strong first-mover advantages over later entrants'. The problem is that, as these organisations 'succeed and grow larger, it becomes progressively difficult for them to enter the even newer small markets destined to become the large ones in the future'.[22]

Although many companies have been unable to cope with the technological innovations that have then proceeded to completely disrupt their markets—Tower Records, Blockbuster Video, Borders bookshops—it is Kodak that is referred to most frequently in this context. This is in no small part due to the fact that it was Kodak who actually invented the digital camera in 1975. Four years later, a report by Kodak executive Larry Matteson even detailed 'how different parts of the market would switch from film to digital, starting with government reconnaissance, moving on to professional photography and finally the mass market'.[23] As far as companies are concerned, then, the worrying thing about the innovator's dilemma is that it shows how the most successful of businesses can still be brought low by disruptive technologies—and how this can happen even when they are seemingly doing everything right and are managing to accurately predict the future. This is because, while large firms are frequently good at generating innovations that function to sustain their positions in already existing markets, they tend not to be anywhere near so good at responding to innovations with the potential to radically disrupt those markets. In a lecture titled 'Managing Organizational Competence', Rebecca Henderson—who ironically enough served as the Eastman Kodak professor in MIT's management school between 1998 and 2009—provides an illustration of how this situation can occur by imagining the conversation between the person who first developed the digital camera and the Kodak executive they took it to:

> I see. You're suggesting that we invest millions of dollars in a market that may or may not exist but that is certainly smaller than our existing market, to develop a product that customers may or may not want, using a business model that will almost certainly give us lower margins than our existing product lines. You're warning us that we'll run into serious organisational problems as we make this investment, and our current business is screaming for resources. Tell me again just why we should make this investment?[24]

It's not just technologies and markets that can be disrupted by such innovations, though. With the United Kingdom experiencing a prolonged period of economic austerity, the Conservative/Liberal

Democrat coalition government has been emphasising the benefits of private entrepreneurialism, particularly in the high-growth digital sector of the economy, championing the development of a 'Silicon Roundabout' Tech City Cluster in East London. Yet in relation to the amount of income they can generate, digital technology companies actually tend to have very small workforces. As Microsoft partner architect Jaron Lanier notes, prior to its film business being creatively disrupted by the digital camera and mobile phone, Kodak used to have '140,000 really good middle-class employees' at its peak, whereas one of its contemporary equivalents, the Facebook-owned Instagram, when it was sold to Facebook for a billion dollars in 2012 (the year Kodak went bankrupt), had just thirteen.[25] This is what the economist and management consultant Will Hutton, building on the work of Richard Florida, has referred to as the '"Great Reset"—a cull of broadly middle-class jobs with middle-class incomes, but with little current sign of what industries and activities will replace them'.[26]

Since one of the organizations involved in the production of this study is located in the city of Coventry, where the first British motor car was made by the Daimler Motor Company in 1897, perhaps we can take the motor industry as another example with which to illustrate the implications of such a reset: and specifically Google's development of a driverless car. Why is a technology company interested in cars? Partly because cars are one of the places where people are going to increasingly use digital technology in the future (communication and navigation devices, music systems, and so forth); and partly because if they can control the transport system and the data it generates it will be equivalent to controlling the telephone or mobile phone networks. However, if the driverless car does indeed become ubiquitous, a whole host of jobs will soon be more or less extinct: bus, taxi, lorry and de-livery drivers, traffic police, positions at car-parks, petrol stations, and so on. Now, as Hutton points out, when there has previously been a major change in transport, from the horse to the motor engine, for example, then the jobs lost were soon replaced by others created: in the car factories of Armstrong Siddeley, Healey, Jaguar, Riley, Rover, Triumph, etc. But it is hard to envisage what today's equivalent of the car factories is going to be, especially when 3D printing will suppos-edly enable everyone to make their own products without the need of factories or large-scale manufacturing . . . *supposedly.*

High-quality university-level education is thus going to be vital to educate those who are freed (aka rendered unemployed) from their jobs in the large-scale manufacturing industries, service industries, and private entrepreneurial sectors by the destructive innovation wrought by new technologies. And as we have seen, this segment of the population includes large numbers not just of the working classes but increasingly of the middle classes too. The question we are thus faced with is whether these people need to be prepared for those areas of twenty-first-century society where there *may be significant opportunities for employment*. Hutton identifies the following trends in the job market: 'human wellbeing' and the associated 'growth in advising, coaching, caring, mentoring, doctoring, nursing, teaching and generally enhancing capabilities'; 'new forms of nutrition and carbon-efficient energy, along with economising with water, to meet the demands of a world population of 9 billion in 2050'; and 'digital and big data management', together with 'personalised journalism, social media, cyber-security, information selection, software, computer science and digital clutter removal'.[27] Or if conflicts are to be resolved democratically, rather than with police horse charges and arrests, will the maintenance of social order in such circumstances require, as the philosopher Brian Holmes has argued, precisely 'a very large number of professional educators . . . artists and thinkers' who can help people with 'learning to live otherwise'? By this Holmes means 'learning to imagine, desire and put into effect another kind of collective existence', different from an emphasis on production—be it associated with large-scale manufacturing, service industries, private entrepreneurialism, or Hutton's micro-producers (who 'produce goods at prices as if they were mass-produced, but customised for individual tastes'). For Holmes, this state of affairs requires 'large investments in education, *in renewed forms of the humanities* [our emphasis], in cooperative processes, in the maintenance of community and ecology, in the development of a philosophy of coexistence'.[28]

On the account presented above, the university clearly still has an important role to play in the societies of the twenty-first century. But why, as researchers working in media and cultural studies, philosophy, critical theory, media arts, digital culture, and politics, are we making such prominent use of a concept—disruption—that, for all its origins in the ideas of Marx, is far more readily associated with business, management, and the market? We are doing so at Coventry, firstly, because it is impossible to escape the market entirely today—and this is especially true of those of us who work *in* the university. And secondly, because escaping the market would not necessarily be desirable anyway. As Jacques Derrida contends, a distinction needs to be made between 'a certain commercialist determination of the market', with its emphasis on 'immediate monetaristic profitability', *and* a sense of the market as a 'public space', which is actually a 'condition of what is called democracy, the condition of the free expression of any and everyone about anything or anyone in the public space'.[29] Accordingly, the approach we are adopting in relation to disruption involves drawing on theorists such as Marx, Derrida, Foucault, Badiou, and Stiegler to develop a critical and creative approach to management, business, and the market—and with them, to the *becoming business* of the contemporary university. We are taking this approach, not with the intention of somehow leaving capitalism and the market (or the university, for that matter) behind and replacing them with something else, such as 'the commons' or even communism. The problem with such a directly oppositional or dialectical stance is that it risks recreating, albeit in a different form, the very thing one is trying to escape (that is, a system based on hierarchisation and competition, not least in relation to rival systems).[30] Instead, we are adopting Derrida's procedure for reading Hegel's dialectic according to a non-oppositional difference, and following the logic of capitalism and the market through 'to the end, without reserve'—to the point of agreeing with it against itself and, in this way, transforming it radically from within.[31] (Or if you prefer things in language derived from the philosophy of Gilles Deleuze, we are developing immanent forms of critique: critique not so much a negative refusal of contemporary capitalism as an 'affirmative or inventive' means of mutating it.)[32]

What this means as far as disruptive technologies specifically are concerned is that we are conceiving them as forms of what Bernard Stiegler refers to as *mnemonics* (cultural memory), and what Plato described as *pharmaka*, or substances that function, undecidably, as neither simply poisons nor cures. As Stiegler maintains when arguing that the 'task *par excellence* for philosophy' today is the development of a 'new critique of political economy' that is capable of responding to an epistemic environment very different to that known by Marx, this 'economy of the *pharmaka* is a therapeutic that does not result in a hypostasis opposing poison and remedy: the economy of the *phar-makon* is a *composition* of tendencies, and not a dialectical struggle between *opposites*.'[33] Rather than reject or critique such technologies outright, his philosophy suggests we need to explore how some of the *tendencies* of which our current economy of the *pharmakon* is com-posed can be deployed to give these technologies new and different inflections. Just as businesses use disruptive technologies as a form of innovation to create new markets and new value networks, according to Christensen, so we are using them to disrupt dominant understand-ings of business and the market. Disruption here is therefore at least double in nature: it is a means of creating innovation for companies and thus helping to support the creative economy and find new sus-tainable business models so that art and culture, together with their potential transformative effects, can flourish, or at least survive, as public space in the neoliberal era;[34] but it is also a means of generating new forms of critique and of creating different kinds of alternatives. Almost inevitably, the latter are in turn capable of providing a means for creating further business innovation in what amounts to a contin-ual process, cycle, or feedback loop, something that has been captured diagrammatically by Tatiana Bazzichelli in her account of networked disruption in relation to art and hacktivism.[35]

This approach to disruption can take the form of both: studying dis-ruptive technologies, including those associated with telephones, mo-biles, and smart phones (in the Centre for Disruptive Media we have developed a creative archiving and digitisation research strand that includes the digitization of British Telecom's Archive, for example);[36] and experimenting with the development and use of disruptive media technologies, including those associated with open source software, collaborative web tools, open access, and mobile and geolocative me-dia. (Witness our *Living Books About Life* project.[37] This is a series of open access books about life—with life understood both philosophi-cally and biologically—that provide multiple points of interrogation and contestation, as well as connection and translation, between the humanities and the sciences.) Yet the idea for us is also to go *beyond* current definitions of disruptive technologies, with a view to not *just* helping to create new markets by doing things the market does not expect, but also disrupting and displacing the existing markets by ex-ploring new economic models and new economies. At one end of the spectrum this takes the form of experimenting with micro-payments, freemium models and the general shift in digital culture from monetizing content to monetizing experiences. (So the Centre for Disruptive Media's virtual and mobile communications research strand includes *Shakespeare Byte-Size*, a project which has digitised the Shakespeare Birthplace Trust archive—as Coventry is close to Stratford-upon-Avon—using augmented reality encounters with Shakespeare.)[38] At the other end of the spectrum it involves us in a range of activities concerned with online attention economies, freemium models, gift economies, creative media activism and so-called internet piracy. Indeed, one of the main businesses and markets the Centre is involved in disrupting with its experiments into new economies and new economic models is its own: namely, that of higher education and the idea of the university as it currently exists. As this project bears witness, what we are interested in is the future of university teaching, learning, research and publication in the age of disruptive media. We view the emergence of media technologies such as smart phones, tablets, p2p networks and the mobile web as providing us with an opportunity to rethink the university—fundamentally, yet also creatively and affirmatively. In other words, our concern is with how digital media technologies can help us to disrupt some of the university's core foundational concepts, values, practices and genres, both theoretically and performatively. These include the idea of the subject as a static, stable, unitary identity, the indivisible and individualized proprietorial author, the linear argument and text, originality, the finished object, 'fixity', intellectual property, copyright, and even the human. The aim is to produce a counter-model both to the *becoming business* of the contemporary university *and* to what Bill Readings referred to as the 'University of Culture', epitomised for him by the German model Humboldt instituted in the nineteenth century at the University of Berlin.[39]

If one way of doing so would be for us to experiment with acting *something like* pirate philosophers,[40] another is provided by the way the higher educational landscape is currently undergoing what some regard as a revolution and others view as indeed a *disruption*. In the latter case, the challenge is coming not so much from the above-mentioned free, autonomous universities of the anti-austerity protests or the projects developed by those 'graduates without a future', but from a somewhat different, albeit at times related, direction: that of Open Education.

NOTES

1. Andrew Ross, *Nice Work If You Can Get It: Life and Labor in Precarious Times* (New York and London: New York University Press, 2009), 190.
2. Ibid., 202–3.
3. Audrey Williams June, 'Some Papers Are Uploaded to Bangalore to Be Graded', *Chronicle of Higher Education*, April 4, 2010, http://chronicle.com/article/Outsourced-Grading-With-Su/64954/. We would like to thank Pete Woodbridge for drawing our attention to this article.
4. John Morgan, 'Warwick and Monash Team Up for Global Strategy', *Times Higher Education*, February 2, 2012, 6–7.
5. John Henry Cardinal Newman, *The Idea of a University Defined and Illustrated* (London: Longmans, Green, 1907). A full transcription of Newman's *The Idea of a University* is available at http://www.newmanreader.org/works/idea/.
6. Stefan Collini, *What Are Universities For?* (London: Penguin, 2012).
7. Edufactory collective, 'EduFactory Discussion Prospectus', *Edufactory: Conflicts and Transformation of the University*, 2007, http://www.edu-factory.org/wp/.
8. 'South East Has Biggest Share of the Wealthiest Households', *Office for National Statistics*, December 3, 2012, http://www.ons.gov.uk/ons/rel/was/wealth-in-great-britain-wave-2/wealth-of-the-wealthiest--2008-10/index.html; the Resolution Foundation, *Gaining from Growth: The Final Report of the Commission on Living Standards*, October 31, 2012, http://www.livingstandards.org/our-work/final-report. See also the Resolution Foundation, *Squeezed Britain 2013*, February 13, 2013, http://www.resolutionfoundation.org/events/squeezed-britain-2013/.
9. 3cosascampaign, http://3cosascampaign.wordpress.com/.
10. Aditya Chakrabortty, 'Meet the New Breed of Fat Cat: The University Vice-chancellor', *The Guardian*, March 3, 2014, http://www.theguardian.com/commentisfree/2014/mar/03/new-breed-fat-cats-university-boss-vice-chancellors. A list of the total remuneration offered to vice chancellors in the United Kingdom is provided by *Times Higher Education*, April 3, 2014, 37–44.
11. U.K. Ministry of Defence report, *The DCDC Global Strategic Trends Programme 2007–2036* (3rd ed.), March 2007, 96.
12. For more, see MichaelC, 'What Happens When You Privatise Universities: Now on Video From Chile', *The Putney Debator*, October 19, 2011, http://www.putneydebater.com/2011/10/19/what-happens-when-you-privatise-universities-now-on-video-from-chile/, as well as the numerous pieces on 'Universities in Crisis' around the world published in 2010 in *Radical Philosophy*, including: Nashan Coombs, 'Faint Signal: The Student Occupations in California', *Radical Philosophy* 159 (January/February 2010): 66–68; Alex

Demirovi, 'Education is Not For $A£E: Student Protests in Germany', *Radical Philosophy* 160 (March/April 2010): 58–60; Krini Kafiris, 'Violence and the University Sanctuary Law in Greece', *Radical Philosophy* 160 (March/April 2010): 60–62; 'The Damned Disunited: Trouble at the University of Leeds', *Radical Philosophy* 160 (March/April 2010): 63–64. For coverage of the issue in *Mute* magazine, see *Don't Panic, Organise! A* Mute *Magazine Pamphlet on Recent Struggles in Education* (London: Mute Publishing, 2011) and Danny Hayward, 'Adventures in the Sausage Factory: A Cursory Overview of UK University Struggles, Nov. 2010–July 2011', *Mute*, January 25, 2–112, http://www.metamute.org/editorial/articles/adventures-sausage-factory-cursory-overview-uk-university-struggles-november-2010-%E2%80%93-july-2011. The introduction and free EPUB are available at http://www.metamute.org/dpo and http://www.smashwords.com/books/view/49035, respectively. In addition to ongoing coverage of the subject in *Mute*'s editorial archive, earlier analysis of the 'recomposed' university can also be found in Marc Bousquet and Tiziana Terranova, 'Recomposing the University', in Josephine Berry Slater and Pauline van Mourik Broekman, eds. *Proud to Be Flesh: A* Mute *Magazine Anthology of Cultural Politics After the Net* (New York/London: Autonomedia and Mute Publishing, 2009), 447. A further source of excellent coverage and analysis of austerity and student struggle is *Novara*, http://www.novaramedia.com.

13. The Occupy University (http://university.nycga.net/) is based in New York City. Tent City University turned into the Bank of Ideas when it 'repossessed' empty UBS offices, and soon changed name again—to the School of Ideas—when it was evicted and set up in a disused school in Islington (see http://en.wikipedia.org/wiki/Bank_of_Ideas). Online locations for all subsequent incarnations of the project are erratic, with activity now, it appears, occurring on Facebook and Occupy's radio station (at https://en-gb.facebook.com/Tent CityUni and http://occupyradio.org.uk/, under 'Education'). The same picture of instability is the case for Chicago Messhall and the Really Free School, for which name-specific domains appear to have been registered (which in turn imposes unlikely maintenance demands); see messhall.org and reallyfreeschool.org, respectively. At the time of writing, activity for these can be found at http://brianholmes.wordpress.com/2011/06/26/three-crises-30s-70s-today/ and the Twitter account @TheFreeSchool. For further analysis of the mission and trajectory of Occupy's School of Ideas, see Nick Thoburn, 'Minor Politics, Territory and Occupy', in Becoming Impersonal, *Mute* vol. 2, no. 3 (2012), and http://www.metamute.org/editorial/articles/minor-politics-territory-and-occupy. For the Public School, see http://thepublicschool.org/ and chapter 4 of this book, *Open Education*; Workers Punk University, http://www.culture.si/en/Workers%27_Punk_University; Free/Slow University of Warsaw, http://www.wuw-warszawa.pl/wuw.php?lang=eng; and the University for Strategic Optimism, http://universityforstrategicoptimism.wordpress.com/.

14. Dougald Hine, 'The University Project: Five Reasons', *Dougald's Blog*, September 24, 2011, http://rhapsodi.se/blog/?p=8. For the School of Everything, see http://schoolofeverything.com, and for further context on Hine's work, see http://dougald.co.uk/.

15. Alain Badiou, *The Rebirth of History: Times of Riots and Uprisings* (London: Verso, 2012); Manuel Castells, *Networks of Outrage and Hope: Social Movements in the Internet Age* (Cambridge: Polity, 2012); Noam Chomsky, *Occupy* (London: Penguin, 2012); Michael Hardt and Antonio Negri, *Declaration* (Argo-Navis/Kindle Single, 2012); Endnotes, 'The Holding Pattern: The Ongoing Crisis and the Class Struggles of 2011–13', in *Endnotes #3: Gender, Race, Class and Other Misfortunes* (2013).

16. See, for example, the poster at http://www.flickr.com/photos/34098908@N00/5816327472/.

17. As has been pointed out, 'this in no sense implies that complacency rather than urgency is the appropriate pathos for writing about these matters, but that the urging of urgency maintains a relation to complacency that is not here thought through, just because of the urgency of the argument' (Geoffrey Bennington, 'Emergencies', *Oxford Literary Review*, vol. 18, nos 1-2 [1996]: 201).

18. Maurice Merleau-Ponty, 'Sartre, Merleau-Ponty: Les Lettres d'une rupture', *Magazine Littéraire*, no. 320 (April 1994); cited in Wendy Brown, *Politics Out of History* (Princeton and Oxford: Princeton University Press, 2001), 43.

19. Michel Foucault, 'The Concern for Truth', in Lawrence D. Kritzman, ed. *Politics, Philosophy, Culture: Interviews and Other Writings, 1977–1884* (New York: Routledge, 1988), 263. For a discussion of the importance of the distinction between 'for' and 'in terms of', see Wendy Brown, *Politics out of History*, 42–43.

20. For more on the marketisation and businessification of the university, see David J. Blacker, *The Falling Rate of Learning and the Neoliberal Endgame* (Winchester: O Books, 2013); Andrew McGettigan, *The Great University Gamble: Money, Markets and the Future of Higher Education* (London: Pluto Press, 2013); and Gary Hall, 'Pirate Radical Philosophy', *Radical Philosophy: A Journal of Socialist and Feminist Philosophy*, 173 (May/June 2012), http://www.radicalphilosophy.com/commentary/pirate-radical-philosophy-2. It was in the latter text that some of these questions concerning how we might struggle against the becoming business of the university were first raised.

21. For Marx and Engels, 'conservation of the old modes of production' was the 'first condition of existence for all earlier industrial classes'. By contrast, the bourgeoisie 'cannot exist without constantly revolutionising the instruments of production, and thereby the relations of production, and with them the whole relations of society' (Karl Marx and Friedrich Engels, *The Communist Manifesto* [1848], in *Marx/Engels Selected Works*, vol. 1 [Moscow: Progress

Publishers, 1969]; available as *Manifesto of the Communist Party by Karl Marx and Frederick Engels*, Marxists Internet Archive, 16, http://www.marxists.org/archive/marx/works/1848/communist-manifesto, accessed May 28, 2014).

22. Clayton M. Christensen, *The Innovator's Dilemma: When New Technologies Cause Great Firms to Fail* (Cambridge, MA: Harvard Business School Press, 1997), xix–xx.

23. John Naughton, 'Could Kodak's Demise Have Been Averted?', *The Observer*, January 22, 2012, http://www.theguardian.com/technology/2012/jan/22/john-naughton-kodak-lessons.

24. Rebecca Henderson, 'Managing Organizational Competence', MIT Sloan School of Management, http://web.mit.edu/rhenders/www/Teaching/day2a_jan05.ppt.

25. Jaron Lanier, 'The Internet Destroyed the Middle Class', *Salon*, May 12, 2013, http://www.salon.com/2013/05/12/jaron_lanier_the_internet_destroyed_the_middle_class/; see also Jaron Lanier, *Who Owns the Future?* (New York: Simon and Schuster, 2013), xii.

26. Will Hutton, 'Driverless Cars, Pilotless Planes . . . Will There Be Any Jobs Left for a Human Being?', *The Observer*, May 19, 2013, 28, http://www.guardian.co.uk/technology/2013/may/19/driverless-cars-pilotless-planes-jobs-human; Richard Florida, *The Great Reset: How New Ways of Living and Working Drive Post-crash Prosperity* (New York: Harper, 2010).

27. Will Hutton, 'Driverless Cars, Pilotless Planes', 28.

28. Brian Holmes, 'Driverless cars, pilotless planes—will there be jobs left for a human being', <nettime-l> mailing list, May 25, 2013, http://nettime.org/Lists-Archives/nettime-l-1305/msg00042.html.

29. Jacques Derrida, in Jacques Derrida and Bernard Stiegler, *Echographies of Television* (Cambridge: Polity, 2002), 47, 83, 44.

30. Even the notion that the theory of disruption has been debunked by Jill Lepore can be seen as part of the cycle of market innovation by which we are constantly encouraged to move on to the next new thing and leave the now old and unfashionable behind: the latter taking the form of the theory of disruption itself in this case. And that is before we even begin to address the fact that what Lepore challenges is not so much the idea that capitalism develops by 'constantly revolutionising the instruments of production' (that the emergence of digital photographic technology has 'creatively disrupted' the analogue photographic industry, say). What Lepore discredits is the rigour of Christensen's research regarding the handpicked case studies he uses to demonstrate his concept of the 'innovators dilemma', on the grounds that many of the companies that are his case studies are selectively chosen and don't match his theory. See Jill Lepore, 'The Disruption Machine: Why the Gospel of Innovation Gets It Wrong, *The New Yorker*, June 23, 2014, http://www.newyorker.com/reporting/2014/06/23/140623fa_fact_lepore?currentPage=all.

31. Jacques Derrida, 'From Restricted to General Economy: A Hegelianism Without Reserve', *Writing and Difference* (London: Routledge and Kegan Paul, 1978), 260.

32. Brian Massumi, *Parables for the Virtual: Movement, Affect, Sensation* (Durham, NC, and London: Duke University Press, 2002), 17.

33. Bernard Stiegler, *For a New Critique of Political Economy* (Cambridge: Polity, 2010), 11, 43. For more of this reading of Stiegler, especially in relation to his concept of technogensis and argument for 'a generalised technicity', see Gary Hall, '#MySubjectivation', *New Formations*, 79, Autumn 2013, http://www.lwbooks.co.uk/journals/newformations/pdfs/nf79%20hall.pdf.

34. Our thanks to Karen Newman for emphasizing the importance of this point.

35. Tatiana Bazzichelli, *Networked Disruption: Rethinking Oppositions in Art, Hacktivism, and the Business of Social Networking* (Digital Aesthetics Research Center, Aarhus University, 2013), 10. For Bazzichelli, 'the goal is not to frontally oppose the adversaries, but to trick them by "becoming them", embodying disruptive and ironic camouflages. Bypassing the classic power/contra-power strategy, which often results in aggressive interventions that replicate competitiveness and the violence of capitalism itself, to apply disruption as an art form means to imagine alternative routes based on the art of staging paradoxes and juxtapositions. Disruption becomes a means for a new form of criticism' (12).

36. See http://www.coventry.ac.uk/research/grand-challenge-initiatives/grand-challenge-initiatives-digital-media/projects/bt-digital-archive/.

37. See http://www.livingbooksaboutlife.org/.

38. See http://citylabcoventry.org/cityprojectarticle.asp?slevel=0z0&parent_id=1&renleewtsapf=39.

39. Bill Readings, *The University in Ruins* (Cambridge, MA, and London: Harvard University Press, 1996).

40. Hall, 'Pirate Radical Philosophy'.

2

❖ ❖

A Radically Different Model of Education and the University

A number of factors are today making possible what for decades could only be dreamt of: the widespread provision of free, online, Open Education, and Open Educational Resources,[1] regardless of a student's geographic location, personal or financial status, or ability to access the conventional institutions of learning—to identify just some of the typical barriers to learning as they have been traditionally construed. A currently emerging consensus—backed by large amounts of state, venture, and philanthropic capital—is that this long-cherished, and ostensibly utopian, vision is now finally achievable thanks to the ubiquity and pervasiveness of the internet and social media. Through the mobile web, self-appointed students across the world can, it is argued, access the kind of high-quality educational materials that were previously only available to a select few. A diverse infrastructure of elite universities, distributed online learning spaces, Open Education projects, and newly created start-ups is rushing to provide these materials. Among enthusiasts—and those who finance their efforts—the global vision is for a wholesale capacity increase in skills and human capital: lifelong learners will chart their own way through their educational experience along what might be described as 'on demand' lines determined by need and desire.[2] An advocacy video titled 'Game Changer: Open Education is Changing the Rules' would even have us all, as potential participants and beneficiaries of the Open Education phenomenon, become 'game-changers'. Over-determined by strategic objectives as this video may be, it captures well the zeal of what is often, and mistakenly (given its lack of a real popular base and its at least partial engineering from above), dubbed the Open Education 'movement'.[3]

Admittedly, when it comes to Open Education, the full sound and fury of what, to date, has been a predominantly North American phenomenon has yet to truly hit the United Kingdom and its £18.7 billion annual revenue stream. There can be little doubt, however, that its tidal wave will arrive soon, in some shape or form. Edinburgh University, for example, has partnered with American venture Coursera to provide a number of Open Education courses; while FutureLearn, a private, for-profit Open Education company and wholly owned subsidiary of the Open University, went live in September 2013 and at the time of writing possesses twenty-six partners, being mostly U.K.-based cultural and HEIs (including the British Library, British Museum and British Council, King's College, London, The University of Nottingham and Trinity College Dublin).[4] Open Education stands, then, to play a significant part in the turbulent times ahead for British universities, which are already grappling with government funding cuts, new charging and financing regimes designed to bring private funding into the higher education sector, indebted and financially insecure students, and the emergence of a myriad of new 'competitors' from both inside and outside of academe.

Within this context, it is the way institutions engage with the expansion of Open Education, as well as the manner in which they handle some of the profound contradictions inherent in the Open Education movement, that may present them with not just the greatest opportunities, but also the greatest threats. Our argument in this book is that, as well as providing a chance to experiment, critically and creatively, with the institution of the university, Open Education also represents a direct challenge to the future of the academic institution.

In the current climate of 'austerity' Open Education can no doubt be used as support for disinvestment in 'bricks and mortar'. Given the financial squeeze universities are suffering, it perhaps should come as no surprise that Open Education is being characterised as offering greater openness, efficiency and cost-effectiveness; as being the harbinger of new income generation opportunities and unparalleled reach; as, in short, being able to act as that magic combination of a cost-saving, revenue-generating vehicle. For example, Open Education can be taken as meaning students can live and study at home—an increasingly attractive option given the global reach of the current economic crisis—yet still get a degree from a prestigious U.S. or U.K. university; but also that fewer academics (including fewer full-time permanent staff) will be needed to teach such students, with some of their functions (including research) being outsourced to parts of the world with low labour costs; and that those faculty who are still needed can do much of their work from home, thus saving on building, library and office space, heating, lighting, electricity and all the other infrastructural costs involved in running and maintaining a bricks-and-mortar campus. Certainly, it is not hard to envisage Open Education–supportive government policies, coupled to an increase in digital provision, leading to an educational landscape with fewer HEIs due to the notional reduction of 'building based' needs. Based on recent trends, there is also a danger of Open Education becoming a skills/numbers/targets generator, much like the U.K. Apprenticeships scheme: funded to nurture a dramatic, generalised hike in teaching provision, while in reality leaving a human skills capital deficit in its wake. Yet as David Golumbia emphasises with regard to the situation in the United States, there can be detected in Open Education a still greater threat:

> The neoliberal assault on higher education . . . exists primarily to limit the amount of critical thinking that goes on in the minds of citizens, because democratic thought, with its emphasis on critique, has become a major stumbling block to capital's pure accumulation and acceleration. More accurately: it is one of the only remaining stumbling blocks to capital's accumulation. . . . The instrumentalization and corporatization of the University is one of the primary tactics this assault uses to realize its strategy, and thus analyses that attempt to meet the assault halfway by assessing liberal arts education on the basis of measurable outcomes . . . can only add fuel to the fire that is meant to burn down the University's most vital function: the maintenance of democracy through the continued study of the many discourses . . . that have gone into its development.
>
> Given the above, it is vital for educators to realize that the advent of massive online education environments, including MOOCs, is not being done primarily to 'democratize' access to education, but instead as the decisive tactic in the war to analyze forcibly each part of higher education on instrumental and economic terms.[5]

Open Education's explicit (and often deliberate) fusion of conservative, liberal, neoliberal, and more radical tendencies and discourses is undoubtedly an important element in this somewhat contradictory and confusing picture. In this sense, the near-ubiquitous talk of 'Edupunks', 'DIY Universities', and the 'hacking' of fusty departments can also appear as little more than a necessary first building block in the construction of new kinds of academies, accreditation systems, syllabi and assessment procedures that are *different yet the same.*[6] A certain amount of creative disruption is a necessary part of the process of delivering the new (albeit more instrumentalised, corporatised and less critical) Ivy League and Russell Group, it seems.

Of course, to some extent a tension between conservative *and* progressive tendencies was always present in the university. But the *at least double* nature of the situation now appears rather pronounced, contributing to an inescapable sense that all is not quite what it seems with Open Education. Viewed in this light, a lack of rigorous critical engagement with Open Education's core precepts can represent a serious problem. Consequently, in what follows, we argue that one way of responding to the rapidly changing higher education environment is by creating spaces for just such a critical engagement. We see this as an important part of a broader educational strategy for proactive experimentation with new and emerging 'open' media, designed to generate possibilities for a radically different model of the university.

NOTES

1. The term Open Education (OE) can be understood as referring to a broad network of endeavors to provide open access to educational engagement and experience; Open Education Resource (OER) was defined as the umbrella term for digital learning at the 2002 UNESCO conference on development in the Global South. In the Academic Partnerships White Paper, 'Making Sense of MOOCs: Musing in a Maze of Myth, Paradox and Possibility', 2012, http://www.academicpartnerships.com/sites/default/files/Making%20Sense%20of%20MOOCs_0.pdf, John Daniel has provided a brief history of the term Open Educational Resources (OER) as follows:

> From the late 1990s MIT had experimented with putting materials associated with its credit courses on the web for free. This was announced as the MIT OpenCourseware project in 2002. Later the same year, at a UNESCO Forum on the Impact of Open Courseware for Higher Education in Developing Countries, the term Open Educational Resources was coined as a generic term for such developments.

2. See Daniel E. Atkins, John Seely Brown, and Allen L. Hammond, *A Review of the Open Educational Resources (OER) Movement: Achievements, Challenges, and New Opportunities*, a report to the William and Flora Hewlett Foundation, February 2007, http://www.hewlett.org/uploads/files/ReviewoftheOERMove ment.pdf. The project continues at http://www.oerderves.org/. The foundation describes itself as the lead grant maker in the area of OER and has, since 2001, financed or co-financed over fifty key strategic initiatives in the field, including MIT OpenCourseWare and the Creative Commons. Documents on its OER Initiatives and most recent Strategic Plan express well its vision of the role OER are to have at a global level, particularly vis à vis the Global South. See http://www .hewlett.org/uploads/files/OER_overview.pdf and http://www.hewlett.org/ uploads/documents/Education_Strategic_Plan_2010.pdf.

3. 'Game Changer: Open Education Is Changing the Rules', June 5, 2012, http://www.youtube.com/watch?v=6Z7kEgIGVKQ.

4. FutureLearn was launched by the Open University's vice chancellor, the ex-Microsoft general manager and Thomson Learning employee, Martin Bean. As we noted earlier, Bean was the highest paid vice chancellor in the United Kingdom at the time of writing.

5. David Golumbia, 'Executives and Corporatization', empyre mailing list, November 25, 2012. See also Golumbia's blog post, 'Centralization and the "Democratization" of Higher Education', *Uncomputing*, November 9, 2012, http://www.uncomputing.org/?p=160.

6. See Anya Kamenetz, *DiY U: Edupunks, Edupreneurs, and the Coming Transformation of Higher Education* (Vermont: Chelsea Green, 2010), which is also part of a blog project at http://diyubook.com. For a British take, see 'Hacking the University', an SXSW workshop organised by Clare Reddington from the Bristol-based media centre Watershed: http://panelpicker.sxsw.com/ vote/2081.

3

❖ ❖

The Educational Context

GLOBALISATION AND THE 'LEARNING REVOLUTION'

Higher education has reflected, or indeed, facilitated, the influences of globalisation for decades, if not centuries. Within the current generation, the courting of international, fee-paying students, the initiation of international franchises, partnerships and 'systems', as well as the development of (long-)distance learning packages testify, in a variety of ways, to the steady enlargement of the operational terrain of individual HEIs—what would today be called their 'market'. Over the past several years, however, a phase shift has occurred in this process of enlargement. Educational-institutional development models are now perceived as having to be, *in principio*, oriented towards the global horizon, its new opportunities and markets—often as a thinly disguised panacea for problems these models of educational-institutional development cannot even begin to 'solve' from home. While the turn towards global 'competitiveness' and client 'acquisition' might be adequately captured by descriptors like the 'neoliberalisation' and 'businessification' of educational institutions, the factors determining this change, or acceleration, are varied and multiple. To provide what are only the most obvious examples, they include global economic, social and governmental trends, the onward race of technology, growing infrastructural capacity, corporate concentration of capital, transnational rights-based agreements and goals on provision. They are also heavily affected by local context. In fact, due to the complexity of the issue, it often appears impossible to say just which constituency it *is* exactly that is in overall command or leading change. (Indeed, it might be said that, often, no one *is* fully in charge of what is a heavily overdetermined situation.)

It is also important to note that, increasingly, the long- and even short-term teaching and learning 'strategies' adopted by HEIs are defined by one of the most opaque areas of academic governance: the relationship between vendors, IT staff, finance and legal staff. Implementing systems that merely comply with diverse legal requirements (privacy, intellectual property, and security) is a backwards-compatible strategy, and minimising 'support' demands is in itself a daunting task. In such a context, 'innovation' of almost any flavour is widely perceived in pessimistic terms—as risk. As a result, IT in higher education is often shaded with extremely conservative stances.

'Telepresent' learning, meanwhile, has become such a common cultural vernacular that the term should probably be dismissed as quaint. Endlessly fussing with gadgets and systems is 'ubiquitous' or 'pervasive'; and explaining how to resolve this or that problem—with a device, a procedure, a department, an organisation—has become, for many, second nature. Instructional videos on almost any and every subject imaginable, sometimes quite complex and procedural, are available on sites such as YouTube and Instructables.com. Yet beneath these overt forms there lie oceans of documents that are not typically recognised as 'instructional', such as video-game walkthroughs and 'cheats,' FAQs, how-tos, discussion forums, 'tips' and 'tricks', guides, and so on. The applied nature of these resources no doubt helps shape, perhaps decisively, the ways in which explicitly educational materials are received—for example, by providing a wealth of para-pedagogical examples and contributing to the expectation that these materials should enable the student to *do something easily*.

As far as the feared exodus from the university proper—let alone 'Real Life' (RL)—this might illustrate, the *Open Educational Practices and Resources: OLCOS Roadmap 2012* document, edited by Guntram Geser in 2007, already speaks of students feeling 'powered down' when they enter the classroom and hand in their work.[1] The teachers consulted for the report perceived their students as deflated by the lack of connectedness—and, in the case of submitted work, by speaking to an audience of one when their social media activity outside the classroom reached so many more than that. The question is: Do the seemingly 'peripheral' and 'non-intellectual' para-pedagogies that shape students' expectations of teaching and learning offer a more productive and applicable model than many educators are ready—or willing—to acknowledge? Or are they part of the de-territorialising of higher education? And, more to the point in this context, do they offer useful examples for educators in the academy? What at this moment of enormous turbulence—wherein Open Education threatens to break the banks of the university and escape it entirely—can the inherent particularities of HEIs still offer?

At issue is not so much 'catching up with the kids'. It is rather that the academy as an institution can *learn along with them* by analysing and adopting fruitful techniques, often from non-obvious contexts. Academia is plagued by tendentious confusions concerning expertise in the subject matter and material versus expertise in teaching: lots of people know X or Y but are uninspiring teachers. The 'pedagogical' or 'educational turn' coursing through contemporary art and culture offers a fertile field for disentangling some of these confusions, and for those teaching in universities to learn new and alternative ways of 'delivering' knowledge. Or rather, opportunities have now arisen for including pedagogical and curricular models that perceive education in a radically different way: that is, as not simply being about 'delivery' or even established 'knowledge', but rather about a distinctly social and relational process that is now distributed across and between physical and online spaces.[2]

THE OPEN EDUCATION LANDSCAPE

In our pursuit of this idea of education as a social and relational process, our own thinking on the subject has been framed by a number of tendencies and phenomena that can be broadly observed within the Open Education landscape at the moment. Since they do not form our main topic of concern here we have decided to provide just a brief introductory overview in the section that follows, so as not to delay the reader's progress to the main thrust of our argument any more than is necessary. This overview has been created by summarizing these tendencies and phenomena and grouping them into four areas, listed in bullet point format for ease of reading. The four areas in question are: the student, the university, and knowledge; online learning and social media; IPR and piracy; and the open access movement.

THE STUDENT, THE UNIVERSITY, AND KNOWLEDGE

Observable tendencies and phenomena within the Open Education landscape in this area include:

- A dramatic increase in student mobility, resulting in global 'shopping' for education (the recent tightening of U.K. visa restrictions notwithstanding).
- The normalisation of university-level fee-paying study, and state inculcation of *massive* student debt. U.S. student debt in 2012 was estimated to be over $1 trillion. The size of the British student debt is currently £46 billion, but it is estimated to rise to £200 billion by 2042, with the increase in student fees and adverse employment conditions both cited as reasons for the escalation. In late November 2013, it was announced that part of the student loan book was to be sold off, triggering protests over fears that, once held in the private sector, the security of interest levels might reduce and collections would be more aggressively enforced (see chapter 1).[3]
- The large-scale and systematic articulation of higher education specifically, and education generally, to the economic sphere—although not a new phenomenon this articulation has been magnified by the focus on intellectual labour and the so-called 'knowledge economy' (see chapter 1).
- State and corporate investment in lifelong learning agendas and programmes oriented at human capital expansion and economic growth. Parallel state disinvestment in academic learning (particularly the arts and humanities), and even in STEM (science, technology, engineering, and mathematics) subjects, coupled with a movement away from what has been dubbed 'blue-sky' or 'curiosity-driven research' (that is, research with no immediate commercial potential or market application).

- General anxiety over academic freedom (witness the recent launch of the Council for the Defence of British Universities),[4] and the 'purpose' of a variety of subjects, ranging from philosophy and medieval history to the more esoteric corners of science.
- Social struggles around cuts in public funding for education. Street demonstrations, university occupations, and political campaigns have usually been grouped around 'anti-cuts' messages which uphold university education as a public good—and generally construe it as an essential function of the welfare state. But as mentioned earlier, struggles have also protested the role of the university as a 'knowledge factory', with specific objections being to standardisation (the Bologna process), services outsourcing, and a general ceding to profit-led conceptions of education and knowledge.[5]

ONLINE LEARNING AND SOCIAL MEDIA

Observable tendencies and phenomena within the Open Education landscape in this area include:

- The deep penetration of social and mobile media into everyday life.
- A proliferation of online education tools and 'virtual learning environments' (to be used in public and private, open and closed settings).
- The accelerated provision and uptake of tele-present online learning offers, including both cMOOCs and xMOOCs. Although they are very much in the media at the moment, MOOCs are a relatively new phenomenon, as we shall see below, the first explicitly designated MOOC course only appearing in 2008. Consequently, while a number of academics are now studying the MOOC phenomenon, there are as yet relatively few extended, rigorous academic studies available on the subject, and even fewer still on the 2012 batch of so-called xMOOCs (MITx, Udacity, et al.). As our bibliography reflects on occasion, most of the available material is in the form of reports, blog posts, and press articles—and even then many of the latter can often appear as little more than promotional vehicles.

However, Daniel again provides a usefully concise account: both of
the differences between cMOOCs and xMOOCs—'the pedagogical
style of the early courses, which we shall call cMOOCs, was based
on a philosophy of connectivism and networking . . . [as] distinct
from the xMOOCs now being developed by elite US institutions
that follow a more behaviourist approach' (Daniels, op cit., p. 2)—
and of the history of their development.[6]

- A surge of interest in, and research funding dedicated to, pedagogic models which 'blend' the classroom environment with
computer mediated, or online, environments ('blended learning',
'event based learning', 'learning in Second Life', the 'flipped classroom', and so forth).
- The proliferation of non-academic open learning environments,
including:

  - self- and peer-organised learning (for example, The Public
School—see chapter 5).
  - wiki-esque or crowd sourced learning platforms, funded by private capital, for collaborative self-education on general knowledge (for example, Quora).
  - 'public good' and commercial learning platforms, with newly
originated content (for example, Khan Academy and Udacity—
see chapter 5).
  - corporate open media education projects with secondary objectives or 'ulterior motives' (recruitment, content crowd sourcing,
and so on) (for example, YouTube Creator space—see later in
this chapter).

'OPEN' IPR AND PIRACY

Observable tendencies and phenomena within the Open Education
landscape in this area include:

- The increasing uptake of Creative Commons licensing as a public
domain, open content legal framework for publishing and sharing
cultural and educational content. This has seen Creative Commons steadily permeate nearly all Open Educational Resource

(OER) initiatives (not to be mistaken with Open Education initiatives, whose formats are in many cases not re-usable). (For more on Creative Commons, see our passage on Creative Commons Critique in chapter 5.)

- Mainstream promotion of 'culture sharing', 'collaborative working' and 'open knowledge' models by individual advocates and lobbying bodies promoting an 'open internet'. (Cf. Clay Shirky on the SOPA/PIPA [Stop Online Piracy Act/Protect IP Act] bills.[7] For more on corporate lobbying for an 'open internet', see the section on Google's Creator space in the commercial interests section below.)
- The continuing robust health of major players working within traditional, closed IPR or proprietary-infrastructure models, together with the embeddedness of restricted IPR in the nooks and crannies of public culture and broadcast institutions (in museum image repositories; image, film and text content databases; etc.).[8]
- Struggles over piracy, including take-downs of file-sharing sites and related arrests (for example, the charges brought by the U.S. government against the self-declared open access guerrilla, Aaron Swartz, for his alleged large-scale unauthorised downloading of files from JSTOR academic database, which many believe led to his suicide in January 2013; and the earlier closure in 2012 of the Megaupload website and arrest of its founder, Kim Dotcom, for copyright infringement).
- The major, de facto role of piracy in access to educational and cultural materials in the 'emerging economies' of the Global South.

THE OPEN ACCESS MOVEMENT

Observable tendencies and phenomena within the Open Education landscape in this area include:

- The 'Academic Spring': after years of lobbying, the open access movement in academe has recently achieved some important victories against proprietary publishing. At the beginning of 2012, 12,000 academics signed a public petition pledging not to support Elsevier journals, either by publishing in them or by

undertaking editorial and peer-review work for them, unless
the publisher withdrew its support for the Research Works Act,
aimed at curbing government mandated open access policies in
the United States.[9]

- U.K. and EU endorsement of open access: the United Kingdom
  and the European Union are simultaneously also now supporting
  open access policies and although these do not bring about the
  exact changes that many of the wider academic and public interest
  lobby groups are looking for, such developments show that there
  is a significant ground swell of change under way.

  ○ On 16 June 2012, the U.K. government announced an open ac-
    cess publishing policy via Research Councils U.K. (RCUK). The
    policy can be classed as falling under the category of a variant of
    gold open access (publishing in open access journals),[10] where
    Article Processing Charges (APCs) are incurred by academ-
    ics having their papers peer reviewed, edited and made freely
    available online (these are typically around £2,000 per article).
    RCUK's policy announcement was informed by the Finch Re-
    port,[11] which looked to find a balance between all the relevant
    stakeholders involved in the open access debate—apparently
    settling on this intermediate position of APCs to avoid a whole-
    sale reversal of the economic model that has, to date, governed
    academic publishing. However, it is widely held that a move to
    full green open access (which allows academics to self-archive
    their research and publications in central, subject or institution-
    ally based repositories) stands to take place over the coming
    years as a result of market pressures on price, and in order to
    bring the United Kingdom into line with the green open access
    policies that are being developed elsewhere, not least by the
    Obama White House in the United States.
  ○ RCUK also announced that after April 2013 it would use a block
    grant funding mechanism to support the implementation of its
    open access policy.[12] The block grants fund APCs and support
    the recommendation of the Finch Report for gold author-pays
    open access publishing. The House of Lords Select Committee
    on Open Access did however criticise RCUK on the grounds
    that it 'did not consult or communicate effectively with key

stakeholders in the publishing and academic communities when implementing its open access policy'. The committee asked RCUK to 'commit to a wide ranging review of its policy in 2014, 2016 and before it expects full compliance in 2018', because of what it considered an 'unacceptable' lack of clarity in RCUK's original open access policy.[13]

° A February 2013 consultation document from HEFCE concerning the role of open access publishing in the submission of outputs to the post-2014 Research Excellence Framework (REF) did not express a preference for either green or gold open access.[14] European Union statements of the same period indicate a comparable approach (Horizon 2020—The EU Framework Programme for Research and Innovation, 2014–2020): with the European Union's new R&D framework, Horizon 2020, falling into place in 2014, a clear commitment has been made to open access research publishing which, as a direct consequence, also affects U.K. government policy and public funding paradigms.[15] Indeed, the European Commission has proposed that open access will be the general principle for research funded under Horizon 2020.[16] It also recommended that Member States take a similar approach to the results of research funded under their own domestic programmes. The goal is for 60 per cent of European publicly funded research articles to be available open access by 2016.[17]

° On 6 March 2013 RCUK issued a revision of its open access policy in which it states that, while RCUK prefers gold, either green or gold open access is acceptable.

° On 28 March 2014 HEFCE together with the AHRC and ESRC published details of their new open access policy for research assessments after the 2014 REF. To be eligible for assessment (and funding), this policy requires that, after 1 April 2016, all peer-reviewed manuscripts and conference proceedings be deposited in a subject or institutional repository immediately on acceptance for publication. 'The title and author of these deposits, and other descriptive information, must be discoverable straight away by anyone with a search engine. The manuscripts must then be accessible for anyone to read and download once any embargo period has elapsed'.[18]

COMMERCIAL INTERESTS: WHITHER THE BOOK?

Whether or not we are finally witnessing the much-anticipated evaporation of the book as the primary technology for the transmission of knowledge, we are certainly seeing a number of rather destructive consequences emanating from the digital disruption of the publishing industry, where shake-ups, land grabs and competitive reconfiguration (such as Penguin's merger with Random House in an attempt to contend with Amazon) are now the order of the day.

Italian writer and editor Alessandro Ludovico tracks some of the associated anxieties in his book, *Post-Digital Print: The Mutation of Publishing since 1894*.[19] His chapter 'The Death of Paper (Which Never Happened)', tells of the Parisian cartoonist Villemard imagining in 1910 the classroom of the year 2000. Villemard's postcard series, titled *Villemard 2010—en l'an 2000*, depicts students being taught via headphone, while in the background books are thrown into a grinder that converts them to the required audio material. Ludovico points out that this scenario did not in fact challenge the supremacy of the book, as it would have remained the original source of educational material. But now that screen resolutions are approaching those of paper book technology, many do argue that the only remaining obstacle to enabling a transition from paper to screen is the speed of textual navigation that books allow, and their function as a memory aid (since print still enjoys measurable superiority in these areas—although even that may expire soon). While these changes in educational media forms are not the only issue for higher education, they should be considered pivotal. After all, it is the technologies of writing and printing on paper, and the concepts and values inherited from them (the indivisible and individualised proprietary author, uniform multiple-copy editions, fixity, the long-form argument, originality, author's rights, copyright and so on), that have done so much to shape the institution;[20] and so, as educational 'content' lifts increasingly off the printed page, who can say how things will settle?

One simple way to address this question is to analyse the activity of the major commercial players, whose priorities during this period of change will have dramatic consequences. A cursory glance at the U.K. Association for Learning Technology (ALT) sponsors page shows who the country's major public and private players are in Digital—albeit not quite Open—Education.[21] Adobe, Blackboard, BTL (producers of SecureAssess and OpenAssess), Desire2Learn, Pearson, Microsoft, Google, Intel, among others, are here because they fully understand the enormity of the transformation currently underway in secondary and HEIs (that is, they appreciate the size of the 'opportunity'). A related page on the same site, on a 'large scale curriculum redesign conference' which ALT also hosted, is similarly illustrative,[22] as are the individual PowerPoints relaying stories from Leeds City College provided on the same page.[23] What is under discussion, effectively, is technology's place in large-scale processes of 'change management' within educational organisations. In very significant ways, it is primarily about transfers of capital from one place to another (and instituting management systems that allow these transfers to take place smoothly), and only secondarily (if that) about the provision of a good education to as many students as possible.

In anticipation of more comprehensive surveys, we illustrate our point by highlighting the contradictory manifestations of 'free' educational materials in a news story from 2012. Here we see Google U.K.'s learning venture, Google Academy, launch the Open Education flavoured Creator space programme, with offers of: cash packages of up to $5,000 (for equipment and mentoring); free face-to-face 'peering' support; the use of an international network of 'creator spaces'; and reminders of the 4 million open IPR licensed YouTube videos that might function as creative material. It is widely known that Google recognises that the effect of networks is to drive the price of content IPR to near zero and for value to instead reside in statistical analysis of its use. Maintaining an 'open internet' is pivotal to this strategic agenda, as is the maintenance of sites like YouTube as default distribution platforms. As such, Creator space arguably functioned as a PR front for the incentivisation of talented young media producers to increase the quality, volume and transactional activity within YouTube material.[24] It also makes it logical for Google to be reported to be the main backer of U.K. non-profit lobbying initiative, Coadec ('the Coalition for a Digital Economy'), which is pressing the U.K. government towards open-friendly copyright reform.[25]

NOTES

1. Guntram Geser, ed., *Open Educational Practices and Resources: OLCOS Roadmap 2012* (Salzburg, 2007), http://www.olcos.org/english/roadmap.

2. For an influential example, see Irit Rogoff, 'Turning', *e-flux journal*, November 2008, http://www.e-flux.com/journal/turning/.

3. Thair Shaikh, '"Lost" Student Loans Worth £5bn Are Written Off', *The Independent*, November 28, 2013, http://www.independent.co.uk/student/news/lost-student-loans-worth-5bn-are-written-off-8969066.html; and Patrick Wintour, 'Student Loans Worth £900m to Be Sold Off', *The Guardian*, November 2013, http://www.theguardian.com/money/2013/nov/25/student-loans-sold-off-debt-interest.

4. See http://cdbu.org.uk/?page_id=10.

5. As noted in chapter 1, 'The University in the Twenty-First Century', crucial in this turn to a critique of, and protest against, the privatisation of the university has been a growing sense of solidarity among the student and lower-level teaching body with the (increasingly outsourced) workers that 'service' their educational environment. There is a growing realisation that they share certain conditions of life and also possible futures. The indebted and precarious student, and the overworked junior or mid-level member of staff, stand closer to the unprotected cleaner than to the university manager or successful knowledge economy entrepreneur with whom the restructured university asks them to identify. Further coverage of this tendency, and the most recent campaigns it has catalysed, can be found in Richard Braude, 'Crisis in the Cleaning Sector', *Mute*, December 18, 2013, http://www.metamute.org/editorial/articles/crisis-cleaning-sector. See also *Novara* for a variety of audio and other content, including 'Failure of the 2010 UK Student Movement: A Diagnosis', Ser. 3, Ep. 7, 2013, http://novaramedia.com/2013/11/failure-of-the-2010-uk-student-movement-a-diagnosis/. Of course, it is also important to note that, in a more rigorous schematic of class divisions and labour stratification, the precarity of the cultural or academic worker must never actually be equalised with workers outside of this 'cognitive-labour' category. For recent and older analyses of this tendency, which has made significant inroads in the cultural sector, see Angela Mitropoulos, 'Precari-us?', *Mute*, January 9, 2006, http://www.metamute.org/editorial/articles/precari-us, and Dave Beech, 'Art and the Cognitariat', *Dbfreee*, September 19, 2013, http://dbfreee.wordpress.com/2013/09/19/art-and-the-cognitariat/.

6. Harvard University and MIT have also both recently made available a series of working papers on MOOCs at http://harvardx.harvard.edu/harvardx-working-papers and http://odl.mit.edu/mitx-working-papers/, respectively.

7. Clay Shirky's 'Why SOPA is a Bad Idea' is a twelve-minute TED talk which effectively summarised the scope of effects that an anti-sharing bill

like SOPA (Stop Online Piracy Act) might have; the talk was cited widely and became a call to arms of sorts. *The Guardian* published a text equivalent in its 'Comment is Free' section: see Clay Shirky, 'Sopa And Pipa Would Create a Consumption-only Internet', January 18, 2012, http://www.theguardian.com/commentisfree/cifamerica/2012/jan/18/sopa-pipa-consumption-only-internet.

8. For example, if we are to take the British Museum, British Library, and BBC as bellwethers for attitudes in British institutions built to serve the 'public good', there has yet to be a proper acknowledgement of, let alone turn to, 'open standards' in their copyright model. Initiatives like the Digital Public Space and the Wikipedia offshoot, GLAMWiki, are steps in a new direction in that both simulate open access by creating *cordons sanitaires* of sorts for collaboratively pooled public good content deriving from the output and archives of participating institutions. If anything, though, in their apparently heroic pragmatism, these efforts often better illustrate the complexity and rigidity of the current copyright regimes than they manage to forcefully strike a path in a new direction of openness. See the Digital Public Space, http://futureeverything.org/publications/digital-public-spaces/, GLAM CAMP 12, http://uk.wikimedia.org/wiki/GLAM-CAMP_London_2012, and GLAMWiki 2013, http://uk.wikimedia.org/wiki/GLAM-WIKI_2013. For Jisc's involvement supporting the BBC's Digital Public Space Agenda (which has been spearheaded by Tony Ageh, pioneer designer of the iPlayer and now BBC Controller of Archive Development), see http://www.jisc.ac.uk/inform/inform36/DigitalPublicSpace.html#.Us1U6yiID5k.

9. See http://thecostofknowledge.com/.

10. See the account of the gold road to open access in 'Open Access Journal', Wikipedia, http://en.wikipedia.org/wiki/Gold_OA, accessed May 24, 1014.

11. *Accessibility, Sustainability, Excellence: How to Expand Access to Research Publications*, Report of the Working Group on Expanding Access to Published Research Findings, June 18, 2012, http://www.researchinfonet.org/wp-content/uploads/2012/06/Finch-Group-report-FINAL-VERSION.pdf.

12. RCUK, 'RCUK Announces Block Grants for Universities to Aid Drives to Open Access to Research Outputs', November 8, 2012, http://www.rcuk.ac.uk/media/news/121108.

13. Lord Krebs, Chairman of the House of Lords Science and Technology Committee, quoted in 'Lack of Clarity over Open Access is "Unacceptable"—RCUK Must Clarify and Monitor Its Implementation Closely', www.parliament.uk, February 22, 2013, http://www.parliament.uk/business/committees/committees-a-z/lords-select/science-and-technology-committee/news/open-access-report-published/. The report itself is available at: http://www.publications.parliament.uk/pa/ld201213/ldselect/ldsctech/122/12202.htm.

14. See http://www.hefce.ac.uk/news/newsarchive/2013/name,78750,en.html.

15. Horizon 2020, http://ec.europa.eu/research/horizon2020.

16. European Commission, 'Scientific Data: Open Access to Research Results Will Boost Europe's Innovation Capacity', *Press Release Database*, July 17, 2012, http://europa.eu/rapid/press-release_IP-12-790_en.htm?locale=en.

17. European Commission, 'Commissioner Geoghegan-Quinn Discusses Open Access with Key Stakeholders', Research and Innovation: Press Release, Brussels, September 25, 2012, http://ec.europa.eu/research/index.cfm?pg=new salert&lg=en&year=2012&na=na-250912.

18. HEFCE, 'New Policy for Open Access in the Post-2014 Research Excellence Framework', March 28, 2014, http://www.hefce.ac.uk/news/news archive/2014/news86805.html.

19. Alessandro Ludovico, *Post-digital Print: The Mutation of Publishing Since 1894* (Eindhoven: Onomatopee 77, 2012), http://monoskop.org/images/a/a6/Ludovico,_Alessandro_-_Post-Digital_Print._The_Mutation_of_Publishing_Since_1894.pdf.

20. John Lechte, in a comparison between the philosophy of Bernard Stiegler and that of Gregory Ulmer, is just one of those who have pointed to the connection between the university and the book. Indeed, 'the book and analytical thinking are historically linked' here, the book being the 'actualization of analytical thought': 'Historically, the school and the university have been the institutional expressions of the book. Education in this alphabetic environment has the broad aim of teaching general principles and models, principles and models based in the rational symbolic order, the origin of critique' ('The Who and What of Writing in the Electronic Age', *Oxford Literary Review*, vol. 21 [1999]: 140).

21. 'Sponsoring Members,' *Association for Learning Technology*, https://www.alt.ac.uk/our_sponsors.

22. See http://www.alt.ac.uk/news/all_news/large-scale-curriculum-rede sign-conference-recordings-and-webinar and http://repository.alt.ac.uk/2216/.

23. The materials and recordings of the conference have since been moved to the ALT Open Access Repository: http://repository.alt.ac.uk/2216/2/Howard_Browes_Bob_Harrison_presentation.pptx.

24. Creator space, http://youtubecreator.blogspot.de/2012/07/introducing-youtube-creator-space.html.

25. Andrew Orlowski, 'Why Does Google Lobby So Much?', *The Register*, July 23, 2013, http://www.theregister.co.uk/2012/07/23/google_lobby_why.

4

❖ ❖

Open Education

DESCHOOLING SOCIETY

It is striking how a political discourse which sought to criticise the disciplinary structures of traditional schooling is mirrored, with uncanny similarity, in the Open Education movement. The Open Education promotional video cited in chapter 2 contains all the key messages the movement cherishes.[1] The refrains, voiced by teachers and educators, might have been cribbed straight from Jacques Rancière's *The Ignorant Schoolmaster: Five Lessons in Intellectual Emancipation*; or to go further back, to what has become its companion volume, Ivan Illich's *Deschooling Society*.[2] A libertarian melée of right and left discourses makes modern-day Open Educationalists speak of 'taking learning out of the classroom', 'changing the rules', and, provocatively, to seeing Open Education as 'the new definition of fair'. Knowledge, according to these enthusiasts, 'deserves to be free'.

It is hard not to be swept up by the excitement: Who would want to question the global generalisation of a mission expressed when the Open Education Resources movement's trailblazing institution, MIT, considered how the internet might be used for education?

Use it to provide free access to the primary materials for virtually all our courses. We are going to make our educational material available to students, faculty, and other learners, anywhere in the world, at any time, for free.
A Review of the Open Educational Resources (OER) Movement, 2007[3]

As a variety of national and international, public and private bodies embark on this project, in the chapter that follows we offer a reminder of two of the key elements in Open Education's current rationalization: the beliefs that education is a human right, and that access to subsidised knowledge should be free. After drawing attention to the structural challenge presented by accreditation, we conclude this chapter with a description of self-organised education in its non-idealised state—the *technical diaspora* familiar to anyone working in higher education right here, right now.

WHY OPEN NOW?

Education Is a Human Right

In June of 2012, the world saw the '2012 Paris OER Declaration' formally adopted at the 2012 World Open Educational Resources (OER) Congress, UNESCO, Paris.[4] Minding all prior relevant treaties and declarations on copyright and so on, it recommends that 'States, within their capacities and authority':

- Foster awareness and use of OER
- Facilitate enabling environments for use of Information and Communications Technologies (ICT)
- Reinforce the development of strategies and policies on OER
- Promote the understanding and use of open licensing frameworks
- Support capacity building for the sustainable development of quality learning materials
- Foster strategic alliances for OER
- Encourage the development and adaptation of OER in a variety of languages and cultural contexts
- Encourage research on OER
- Facilitate finding, retrieving, and sharing of OER
- Encourage the open licensing of educational materials produced with public funds

Access to Subsidised Knowledge Should Be Free

Academic publishing has been one of the first places of contestation in
society around Open Education because scholars want their work to be
read, appreciated, and re-used, and this is being hindered by the gatekeeping business models of their publishers. The argument put forward is that the public purse should not be drawn on twice, as happens
when universities pay first for the research to be conducted, and then
a second time to acquire that research in the form of peer-reviewed
journals (and potentially a third time if an idiosyncratic, author-pays
version of gold open access is implemented in the United Kingdom).
As noted previously, Elsevier's €725 million annual profit on its journals alone helped catalyse an 'Academic Spring' in 2012, with more
than 12,000 academics signing a public petition against the publisher.
More recently, there has been a call to boycott both Taylor & Francis
and Routledge if their parent company, Informa plc, does not bring
down its journal subscriptions charges and pay the U.K. Exchequer
the approximately £13 million lost in taxes to the treasury as a result
of its 2009 decision to become a Jersey company domiciled in Zug, the
canton with the lowest rate of taxation in Switzerland.

Significantly, Informa derives over half its total annual operating
profit from academic publishing: £85.8 million in 2010, with its journals alone providing 'gross profit margins of over 70 per cent'.[5] That
compares with 6.9 per cent profit margins generally for 'electricity
utilities, 5.2 per cent for food suppliers and 2.5 per cent for newspa-
pers'.[6] Indeed, there appear to be 'only two other industries where
these sorts of return are on offer: the illegal drugs trade and the delivery of university-level business education'.[7] The argument for opening
up research materials is further supported by the fact doing so has had
a positive, not negative, effect on its reputability if citation and use can
be counted as the key measure.[8]

The Accreditation Problem

Accreditation is the key bargaining chip HEIs continue to hold in the
global learning nexus. It is the one function that all stakeholders (faculty, researchers, students, textbook publishers, and commercial entities) cannot manage without. Up until now it has also withstood digital
disruption, continuing to reside stably in education's value chain, even

as it connects with digital information structures and economies. But the challenges to this state of affairs are growing ever more forceful: one of the most interesting and important, initiated in 2011, comes from Mozilla's Open Badges Research programme. The goal of the project is to make a digital ID system that allows multiple partners to assign verifiable accreditation. Significantly, this can be formal or informal, meaning holding a university degree or being a good barista could both be accommodated.

A summary overview of Open Badges shows it supports peer accreditation (allowing for informal accreditation, and hence suiting blended, informal and lifelong learning); enjoys significant uptake by p2p independent learning ventures (for example, Peer 2 Peer University's School of Webcraft); boasts community support from students and from the millions of Mozilla users; and enjoys backing from the U.S. Department of Education, Google, NASA, and private education providers (for example, O'Reilly). While still new and untested, the secret to the success of Open Badges (and where Mozilla is being particularly strategic) lies in the recognition that an educational landscape that opens up, unbundles, and becomes networked and hybridised, demands new kinds of verification and security—something like an online passport-cum-qualifications wallet. The global ascendance of lifelong learning will obviously only increase the urgency of this requirement. For sceptics, such an over-inclusive system of accreditation will forever remain an anathema; for others, the important question may turn out to be whether Mozilla could keep such a system in the public domain, as opposed to being yet another IT product universities must buy into.[9]

Openness as Self-(Dis)Organisation

As noted above, the risk aversion that characterises IT policy across much of higher education has contributed to a growing dilemma. IT departments initially embraced a number of *essential* services such as 'productivity' software, email, the web, 'learning management systems' (LMSes), and wifi, as well as 'non-user-facing' capacities such as data analytics. Subsequently, however, the vast majority of such departments have tended to focus their attention on operational responsibilities (security, privacy, reliability) that can be centrally organised, closed, and controlled, rather than activities that are far less easily controlled because they are more open, decentralised, and distributed. The latter include the extraordinary range of services that have arisen under rubrics like 'Web 2.0', 'social networking', and collaborative- and 'crowd'-oriented systems. It hardly needs to be said that, for many, these newer services have quickly become a dominant face of internet usage—for which most IT departments are, and will remain, woefully unprepared, both in terms of their technology but also their underlying ethos.

The result is a rapidly growing gap between 'officially' supported services and unofficial experimentation often originating in 'classroom' settings—driven, in no small part, by the much-remarked 'changing media consumption habits' of younger people, including early career (and hence often younger) academics. In these populations, questions about whether some service has been 'officially' adopted by an institution are almost incomprehensible: Gmail and its predecessors (following Hotmail, Yahoo, etc.) are the norm, blogging and tweeting is banal, Facebook (superseding Myspace) is almost unavoidable, 'file-lockers' (Rapidshare, Megaupload, and so on) are a widely used resource, and a shifting mélange of more or less synchronous communication tools (SMS, instant messaging, chat, and so forth) has developed into a complex ecology laden with subtle forms of etiquette.

This 'gap' has generated a good deal of institutional and academic anxiety. But it has also offered a space for unparalleled pedagogical experimentation, both witting and unwitting. On the one hand, faculty complaints about students who 'don't understand boundaries'— because they text or email faculty at inconvenient hours and in non-standard or inappropriate language—have become a widespread academic cliché. On the other hand, in the absence of official open services, and in the face of closed, over-functioned, yet still quite inflexible tools such as Virtual Learning Environments (for example, Blackboard or Moodle), faculty have had a fairly free hand to experiment with a variety of platforms and approaches. In the 'blogging' sphere alone, a litany of sites has seen shifting tides of educational activity: Blogger/Blogspot, Drupal, Expression Engine, Minigroup, Moveable Type, Posterous, Typepad, Wordpress, and Xanga, to name only the dominant platforms. Lists of this kind could be generated across a variety of mainly visual media—video (YouTube, Vimeo, Vine, etc.), presentations (for example, Prezi), image-driven social media (Poster-ous, Tumblr), and so on. And at the extremes are rumours of units 'taught entirely on Facebook', and spectacular reflexive experiments such as the algorithmically graded Fall 2007 'Internet Famo' unit (of-fered by Parsons in New York City).[10]

We could say that this experimentation is 'self-organised', but it would be more meaningful to describe it as self-disorganised. Its fragmentation and the qualitative nature of the resulting 'data' (which would be anecdotal and discursive, were it possible to collect) render it all but impossible to assess. However, rather than admit defeat by the standards of traditional assessment, we believe this tendency should be seen, less as a hopelessly flawed source of data but, instead, more as the de facto start of an irreversible trend: away from 'official' cen-tralised models of educational computation, and towards a technical diaspora in which a plurality of tools and platforms are adopted on an idiosyncratic basis to support a variety of pedagogical approaches and curricular contexts.

NOTES

1. 'Game Changer: Open Education is Changing the Rules', June 5, 2012, http://www.youtube.com/watch?v=6Z7kEgIGVKQ.

2. Jacques Rancière, *The Ignorant Schoolmaster: Five Lessons in Intel-lectual Emancipation* (Stanford: Stanford University Press, 1991); Ivan Illich, *Deschooling Society* (Harmondsworth: Penguin, 1973).

3. See Atkins, Brown, and Hammond, *A Review of the Open Edu-cational Resources (OER) Movement*, http://www.hewlett.org/uploads/files/ReviewoftheOERMovement.pdf.

4. See http://www.unesco.org/new/fileadmin/MULTIMEDIA/HQ/CI/CI/pdf/Events/English_Paris_OER_Declaration.pdf.

5. David Harvie, Geoff Lightfoot, Simon Lilley, and Kenneth Weir, 'What Are We to Do with Feral Publishers?', submitted for publication in *Organi-zation*, accessed through the Leicester Research Archive, http://hdl.handle.net/2381/9689; published in *Organization*, vol. 19, no. 6 (November 2012).

6. Simon Lilley, 'How Publishers Feather Their Nests on Open Access to Public Money', *Times Higher Education*, November 1, 2012, 30–31, http://www.timeshighereducation.co.uk/story.asp?sectioncode=26&storycode=421672&c=1.

7. Harvie, Lightfoot, Lilley, and Weir, 'What Are We to Do With Feral Publishers?'.

8. For a summary of reported studies on the Open Access citation advantage, see Alma Swan, 'The Open Access Citation Advantage: Studies and Results to Date', *Technical Report, School of Electronics and Computer Science*, University of Southampton, February 17, 2010, http://eprints.ecs.soton.ac.uk/18516/. A bibliography of such studies is also available at Stevan Hitchcock, 'The Effect of Open Access and Downloads ("hits") on Citation Impact: A Bibliography of Studies', http://opcit.eprints.org/oacitation-biblio.htm. Regularly updated figures regarding the impact of open access are available on the website of the Open Citation Project, http://opcit.eprints.org/oacitation-biblio.html.

9. See http://openbadges.org/ and https://wiki.mozilla.org/Badges.

10. S. James Snyder, 'Googling for Your Grade', *Time*, December 20, 2007, http://www.time.com/time/business/article/0,8599,1697486,00.html.

5

❖ ❖

Open Education Typologies

I'm not sure we always notice: sometimes when mainstreaming happens we don't recognise it. When did e-learning become part of the fabric of education?

—Amber Thomas, Jisc, Programme Manager, Digital Infrastructure, ALT-C conference September 2012[1]

Globally, there exists a tightly woven network of powerful organisations funding, planning, benchmarking, and assessing the efforts of the Open Education movement. Largely based in the United States, their values and operational models have recently gained significant traction in the United Kingdom and Europe, as has an economic model built more broadly on open—rather than closed—informational resources. Jisc (formerly the Joint Information Systems Committee, or JISC) has been an important U.K. player in this area;[2] less directly instrumental bodies, such as the U.K. government created Open Data Institute (founded in 2012 and co-directed by Sir Tim Berners-Lee), are promoting the opening up of government data into public domain form and now also significantly affect the context in which Open Education currently takes place.[3] The United Kingdom is also home to a number of leading international research bodies and universities that have been advocating and funding activities related to Open Education and Open Educational Resources for over a decade. They include The Wellcome Trust, which in 2012 also adopted a policy whereby all the research it supports has to be made available in an open access publication or repository as a condition of funding,[4] and the Open University (see below). During the ten years between UNESCO's declaration on the underlying drivers of Open Educational Resources at the 2002 Forum on the Impact of Open Courseware for Higher Education in Developing Countries, and the universal adoption of the 'Paris Declaration' on OER at the UNESCO OER 2012 Congress, a drive has persisted within U.K. higher education to sustain an ethical mission to provide 'universal education', and to do so with reference to Open Educational Resources. So in principle, the U.K. context is one that should enable open IPR-based processes to flourish.

An important shift that has been visible in the past ten years is that production and dissemination of Open Education Resources is no longer positioned as a driver for a global parity of provision in education—supporting the 'Global South'. Instead, it acts as a model for how *all* education might be provided. This emerging role for Open Education, which incorporates both conventional universities making open versions of their existing content (that is, Open Educational Resources) *and* some limited moves towards devising new forms of pedagogy and new modes of delivery—the live practice of Open Education—raises fundamental questions about the role of universities as gatekeeper institutions for society's knowledge. In particular, making teaching content available through Open Education Resources implicitly enacts a disruption of the boundaries often placed around conventional research and publication. After all, it would seem perverse to retain the existing institutional paywalls and boundaries around ideas, arguments and research findings when these are construed as 'research', yet make the same material freely available through a parallel activity construed as 'Open Education'.

As we mentioned above, from a certain point of view, the benefits of Open Education as a series of practices, Open Educational Resources as a set of accessible artefacts, and open access policies as a proactive stance on the dissemination and circulation of research and scholarship, would seem to be best enhanced when strongly articulated in a coherent approach. If that is the case then in the United Kingdom at least such an articulation is at most still an aspiration. Indeed, the discussion (or rather hype) surrounding MOOCs as a disruptive potentiality for the United Kingdom has so far been understood as a discrete issue, unconnected to research—except on those rare occasions when

MOOCs have been seen as providing private, for-profit, teaching-only providers with free teaching material, 'without the fixed costs of libraries' or the need to reciprocate by contributing to the curriculum of others in turn, 'since their own research resources, as commercial products, would be behind a paywall'.[5] This disconnect between teaching and research might also be a feature of the United Kingdom's higher education research cycle—a fast approaching deadline for the next research selectivity exercise (the REF or Research Excellence Framework) may well exert a conservative influence with respect to open access innovation, for example, since it is likely to make many academics and institutions whose reputations are sustained by proprietary conceptions of IPR and metric-driven evaluation feel inhibited.

As we have indicated, traditional universities internationally are facing an increasingly turbulent operational environment. Rising costs and reduced personal 'returns' for students have engendered talk of a higher education bubble.[6] Government and public sector deficits are influencing higher education policy in Europe, the United Kingdom, and the United States,[7] as is the global rise of private and online education provision. Taken together, these factors form a broad context within which the debate about Open Education is now being conducted. However, while the discussion orients itself towards the intense gravitational field created by the United States, innovations and responses in all national contexts will necessarily be different. Higher education in the United States and United Kingdom, for example, differs in the higher direct fee costs to U.S. students—even accounting for the UK's 'new funding arrangements' (that is, £9K fees). Further, the United States has a higher reliance on expensive, mandatory core texts; there is a different balance between, and tradition of, public and private HEIs; a closer 'proximity' between HEIs and private enterprise and, crucially, to venture capital; tenure, promotion, and career advancement routes work differently; and there are distinctive attitudes, and indeed dispositions, towards innovation. And that is to name just a few. The particular position, ethos, and reputational dynamics of the elite institutions driving Open Education debates in the United States also need to be taken into account. Harvard, MIT, and Stanford are *not* structural equivalents to Oxford and Cambridge, and are certainly not so with regard to Open Education. Whereas Oxford and Cambridge have been happy for specific departments to undertake small, Jisc-funded Open Educational Resources projects over the last five years, MIT has been developing its OpenCourseWare project for ten years now, and has put many eggs into the basket of the edX initiative. Finally, while the U.K. higher education sector has recently moved considerably towards a more 'American' system in terms of the fee structures, wider funding models, and relationships with business mentioned above, it retains many of its traditional features, being more conservative pedagogically, retaining notions of value resting on established institutional and disciplinary hierarchies, and of course operating within a particular state-private-educational matrix at secondary level.

Two illustrations will help to capture some of these differences. One primary market in which MOOCs might find early traction in the United States is mid-tier universities, which conduct large amounts of relatively standardised teaching, based on generic course textbooks. Each course may require students to buy several 'set' textbooks, purchased at a combined cost of several hundred (usually over a thousand) dollars. A notable recent response across North America is to offer digital textbooks, or collections—some of which are 'open' and collaboratively produced—at low or no cost,[8] as well as public schemes such as those in British Colombia to provide free digital textbooks.[9] In this context, venture capital–backed education start-ups such as Coursera, Knewton, 2U, and Straighter Line[10] perhaps find a more receptive audience and amenable context, since they appear to add further value to pooled resources at relatively low cost. In the case of Coursera, this is brand value—giving access to elite Ivy League content for free. In the case of Knewton and 2U,[11] it is networked teaching content backed by big data analytics and/or learning modelling. So the confluence of high marginal costs to aim at, large pools of content and technical expertise, plus aggressive capital seeking to open up a new Klondike, seems quite particular to the U.S. environment.

December 2012 saw the first explicit response to the American xMOOCs from the higher education sector in the United Kingdom: the FutureLearn venture, coordinated by the Open University. FutureLearn clearly intends to adopt some of the characteristics of the Coursera/edX/xMOOC approaches: for example, leveraging elite brand value into large-scale open provision; using online platforms and collaboratively produced content; enabling 'free' access to Open Educational Resources; and using this provision as a 'taster' (that is, marketing strategy) for established course offers and further brand dissemination. However, FutureLearn is an entirely established, institutional initiative—its partners are the British Library and over twenty British universities.[12] Indeed, this seems to be a somewhat defensive response to the emergence of Open Education at international level, intended to be disruptive of neither the United Kingdom's higher educational infrastructure, its economics, pedagogy, nor even its technological platforms.[13]

The Open University will no doubt seek to leverage its well-established expertise in online distance provision, allied with its more recent developments in Open Educational Resources, based in OpenLearn and SCORE, into a venture that will deliver some U.K. higher education content to the MOOC marketplace. But at this early point FutureLearn evokes nothing so much as a post–social media Universitas 21 Global, itself a flagging consortium which responded to the global education market expansion by morphing into GlobalNxt University.[14] In contrast, edX and Udacity have struck deals with Pearson Education to deliver certification packages, while Coursera, as is well known, is a venture capital–backed spin-out company, led by former Stanford University faculty. In other words, the United Kingdom strains to mimic initiatives which lend strength from a U.S. context that has what appears to be an almost default coincidence of Open Education innovation, a technology-innovations thrust to such development, and an established trend for the outsourcing of educational provision.

Evidently, then, Open Education in the United Kingdom has not yet entered the entrepreneurial era to the degree it has in North America, and the Open Education landscape overall is marked by a series of notable distinctions with particular contexts generating place-specific patterns of development. In this respect, Open Education practices and initiatives should be understood as being more or less disruptive along different axes: some are explicitly intended to challenge existing institutional arrangements and economies per se—or perhaps those of competitor institutions. Others meanwhile are pedagogically and/or technologically radical, and have begun to engender institutional disruptions only indirectly and inadvertently. At one extreme perhaps is FutureLearn, which seems to be intended to bolster existing institutions, operate within known technologies and act as an additional taster for, or route into, established HEI provision. At the other end of the spectrum, while starkly different, both Straighter Line (a start-up rooted in the pragmatic

challenges surrounding attainment and transfer of university credits) and
P2PU (a non-profit deriving both learners and educators from its user
community) are conceived as changing the educational landscape—its
economics, pedagogies, and modes of participation (see figure 5.1).[15]

At this moment in time, U.K. Open Education practitioners probably
have more in common with early North American Open Education
innovators (2000–2008), who usually aspired to develop their pedagogic practices within strong ethico-social frameworks. Their online
teaching/publishing spaces, and later cMOOCs, capitalised on a series
of technological innovations (web, HTML, social media) that arose outside of educational development. These innovators sought to provoke
pedagogic transformation by breaching the boundaries of HEIs, but
principally by developing and extending connectivity amongst the communities of learners. Their models emphasised collaborative production,
sharing, and re-use/re-mixing. Yet these Open Education practitioners
(for example, Dave Cormier, Stephen Downes, Jim Groom, Howard
Rheingold) could also be accused of holding romanticised conceptions
of connectivism and self-organisation, which their MOOCs entail. In
addition, they often articulated what might be dubbed 'techno-booster'
positions, displaying a number of blind spots when it comes to the politics of the key media systems (and the corporations supporting them)
that their approaches rely on. In their view, politics frequently appears
to be something that only happens 'IRL' (in real life), not in the online
spaces it gives rise to and which directly underpin their work.

Compared to the United States of even half a decade ago, there
remains in the United Kingdom the sense of an aspiration towards
systematicity; a quasi-logical progression of structured funding phases
and investment plans; and a self-consciously 'collaborative' network of
institutions working together to achieve the same goal. Government
and certain key strategic funders—primarily Jisc—seek to determine
the shape of the field. Independent activity is scarcely visible, mostly
because it takes place at an extremely modest scale, coming either
from the ground up and from within the context of academic/peda-
gogic innovation, or from the worlds of activist and student struggle,
rather than from highly publicity-savvy start-up and commercial
ventures with serious expansion and marketing plans in place. This
may of course change. At the current moment in time, however, the
U.K. Open Education 'scene', if such a thing exists, is unmistakably

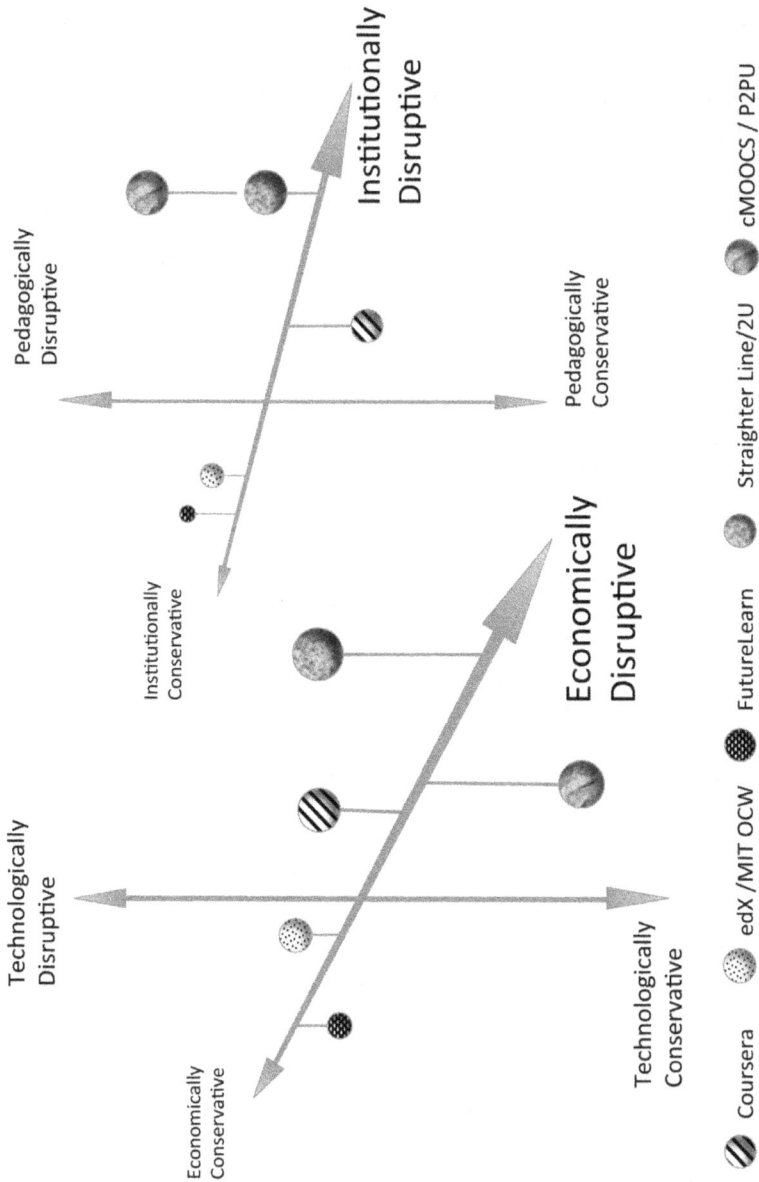

Technologically
Disruptive

Pedagogically
Disruptive

Institutionally
Disruptive

Institutionally
Conservative

Pedagogically
Conservative

Economically
Disruptive

Economically
Conservative

Technologically
Conservative

Coursera   edX /MIT OCW   FutureLearn   Straighter Line/2U   cMOOCS / P2PU

Figure 5.1

reminiscent of early, academic-flavoured internet culture, with all the associated infrastructures and participant demographics one would expect (that is, project managers, academics, data analysts, technologists, and information engineers). It does not yet reflect the diversity of the internet at large which, aside from marking a lack of class, gender, and ethnic diversity, it has to be said, also extends to the absence of aggressive private sector intrusion.[16]

As we described earlier, Open Education practices have from the outset embodied simultaneously progressive, radical, liberal, neoliberal and conservative tendencies. Nevertheless, with new Open Education platforms being launched on what can feel like an almost daily basis, a rough typology is emerging. The promise of MOOCs, for example, is to serve a global community of self-selecting students with what are described as the same quality materials as the originating (or partner) university. Other, newer players—such as Udacity or Khan Academy—originate their own material, independent of (or even in competition with) established HEIs. A variety of charging and certification models are also visible, but the central paradigm is for free access to content and resources and so underlying business models or financial considerations tend to be downplayed. At this point, then, it may be helpful to distinguish these categories, as well as to discuss specific examples, which we do below this group of preliminary categorisations:

- Venture capital–backed educational start-ups which seek to disrupt the established practices, institutions, and economies of higher education. These neoliberal entities develop aggressively market-driven alternatives—some of which have 'open' elements (for example, Straighter Line, 2U).
- Collaborative projects between (largely U.S. Ivy League) universities and private enterprise tech companies that are designed to disrupt other institutions and add resilience and market share to their existing dominance by anticipating market and technology trends globally. These often provide open access to content and passively allow re-use (for example, Coursera).
- MOOC and Open Courseware offerings—similar to the above but distinguishing themselves in being more institutionally located. These are more obviously about leveraging institutional brand

value, but they are also more traditional pedagogically (for example, edX and MIT's OpenCourseWare).

- Educationally innovative, highly connected and distributed online learning spaces, radically committed to Open Education principles, Creative Commons licensing, sharing and re-use, together with collaborative approaches to content generation and learning. These entities often derive educational provision from within universities while existing independent from, and outside of, their institutional boundaries. Their primary concern is to mobilise the benefits of web platforms to leverage educational content into new learning communities (for example, P2PU and early connectivist MOOCs).
- A long-standing tradition of British (and European) Open University Learning offering degree-level education to any of those who want to undertake it (and so are freely accessible irrespective of normal qualifications). The Open University in the United Kingdom offered content first through broadcast media-based, textbooks, remote and local tutoring. This has subsequently become increasingly online distance learning provision. (There are of course open and free universities in this mode across Europe.)
- A recent series of U.K. Open Educational Resources projects supported by higher education funding agencies, government, and charitable foundations—Jisc, HEA, NESTA and TSB. These have been simultaneously both particularistic and part of an attempted overarching policy.

MOOCS

To the degree that the term has become practically synonymous with Open Education, the 'MOOC', or Massive Open Online Course, is, as was noted previously, in fact fairly novel (being coined as late as 2008). As John Daniel has observed:

> The term MOOC originated in Canada. Dave Cormier and Bryan Alexander coined the acronym to describe an open online course at the University of Manitoba designed by George Siemens and Stephen Downes . . . the aim of the course . . . was to follow Ivan Illich's injunction that an educational system should 'provide all who want to learn with access

to available resources at any time in their lives; empower all who want to share what they know to find those who want to learn it from them; and, finally furnish all who want to present an issue to the public with the opportunity to make their challenge known' (Illich, 1971).

We quote Illich to emphasise that the xMOOCs attracting media attention today, which are 'at the intersection of Wall Street and Silicon Valley' (Caulfield, 2012), appear to have scant relation to those pioneering approaches. . . . Surprisingly perhaps, those who coined the term MOOCs and continue to lead much Web discussion about them draw little attention to this change. . . . There seems to be a herd instinct at work as universities observe their peers joining the xMOOCs bandwagon and jump on for fear of being left behind.[17]

At such a relatively early stage of development, both MOOCs' own user projections and their analysis of them still tend towards the anecdotal—and are often extrapolated from non-'massive' sources such as mainstream 'Learning Management Systems' (LMSes) and broader Open Educational Resources (although an increasing number of academic studies of MOOCs are beginning to be conducted).[18] Nonetheless, one could argue that 'massively' might be more accurately stated as 'spectacularly': numbers such as the '160,000 students in 190 countries' who enrolled in Stanford's Fall 2011 Artificial Intelligence course are surely astounding. At the same time, it is reported that at 'Harvard, more people have signed up for MOOCs in a single year than have attended the university in its entire 377-year history'.[19] But examples like this can hardly serve as stable or representative models, in addition to which they stand to evolve, change and diversify at such speed that gauging their performance and 'effectivity' will remain difficult.[20] A recent report, issued by Universities U.K. in May 2013, has been able to offer more exhaustive and comprehensive analysis, but even this cannot escape the basic reality that, so early in their development, MOOCs' long-term claims are by definition untested.[21] If we set aside the 'massive' network infrastructure, which is in no way an intrinsic part of the course itself, a 'MOOC' is just an 'OOC'—a free online open course, accessible to anyone at any time. It is conceivable that, among the 'massive' numbers of students that might enroll in a unit, remarkable new forms of collaboration and co-learning could occur; but it is unlikely that they would do so within the technical confines of a prescribed setting (such as an LMS) or the official duration of the unit.

Even more recently published analysis shows that MOOCs have important work to do separating the wheat from the chaff among student conversations in online fora, which are promoted as a unique and distinctive feature of their learning experience. A University of Pennsylvania Graduate School of Education study of 1 million MOOC users of the institution's sixteen Coursera courses discovered that they have very few active users, with an average completion rate of only 4 per cent across all sixteen courses and only approximately 50 per cent of those registered for a course ever having watched a lecture.[22] Such dramatic non-completion rates as are now widely observable are cited by MOOC students to be partly attributable to their inability to locate what's useful among the chatter (though this is not social, but rather has to do with all participating students needing to familiarise themselves with their new environment, feeling bewildered, asking endless routine practical questions, and so on.).[23] This is not to mention the structural inequalities in education such drop-off rates relate to,[24] the question as to whether the success or failure of MOOCs can be measured according to the same criteria and metrics that are applied to conventional university courses (for example, enrollment and completion rates), or the untransparent ways in which unwitting 'public education' students have been enlisted to the strictly 'private profit' cause of MOOC players like Udacity.[25] Less noted than the 'massive' numbers, yet perhaps more useful in this context, is the experience of the 200 or so Stanford students who enrolled for the 'face-to-face' version of the Artificial Intelligence course: that number quickly shrank to thirty because 'they preferred the online videos, with their simple views of a hand holding a pen, working through the problems'.[26] This points to much more intimate lessons to be learned: subjects that lend themselves to visually oriented pedagogies are likely to prosper in online environments; and, conversely, the visually oriented aspects of many types of courses and units might benefit from being presented online.

In the U.K. context, something similar has been remarked by Central Saint Martins, University of the Arts London, whose project ALTO (a two-year, Jisc-funded initiative under the 'OER3' strand) aims to generate more visually compelling (and thus also arts- and humanities-relevant) material than is routinely available within Open Education environments.[27] Does this indicate that in the future university education may be increasingly visual in nature? The philosopher

Bernard Stiegler has recently gone as far as to argue that, with the web and digital reproducibility, we are living through a 'radically new stage of the life of the mind, whereby the whole question of knowledge is raised anew':

> as with the Bologna University during the 11th century, then with the Renaissance era, then with the Enlightment and Kant's question in Le conflit des facultés, we are living a significant organological change—knowledge instruments are changing and these instruments are not just means but rather shape an epistemic environment, an episteme, as Michel Foucault used to say.[28]

Certainly there are many more lessons to be learned from applied OOC experiences of this kind, however 'massive'. The problem is how to pool those experiences across institutions in ways that would make those lessons visible. As with many Open Education–related issues, it may well be that a key opportunity is secondary, lying not in the direct provision of education to students but, rather, in how the deliberate restaging of particular pedagogical moments can offer useful insights that are broadly applicable across educational environments (for example, in classroom practice and asynchronous online settings). A further problem, however, is that many experiments with (M)OOCs to date have been pedagogically retrograde, often amounting to little more than online broadcasting.

TED

There is a common popular refrain that the TED Conference system ('Technology, Entertainment, and Design') suggests a viable model for large-scale online education. After all, it is argued, its success at showcasing wildly diverse content to audiences around the world—for free—demonstrates both a capacity to present, and a widespread hunger for, inspiring work.

It would be churlish to dismiss the speakers and their work en masse because of the context in which they appear. Nevertheless, it is willfully naïve to think that this model has much to do with education. According to TED 'curator' Chris Anderson (not to be confused with the former *WIRED* editor of the same name), TED's global system 'draw[s] from a pool of ... up to 10,000 [talks] recorded at the various TEDx events around the world, not to mention our other conference partners'.[29] From this, through an opaque and promotionally driven process—one that bears a curious resemblance to television programs such as *X Factor*—they 'post one talk a day on [their] home page.' Speakers are heavily coached, and talks are staged with world-class production values. Presenters are stringently evaluated on their ability to present affirmative, motivational, and 'wondrous' ideas—in no more than eighteen minutes. And while it is clear that TED's programmers are earnestly committed to seeking out demographic diversity among their speakers, diversity stops there. Speakers' narratives and analyses are self-reported; and pessimism, ambivalence, ambiguity and above all politics are weeded out at every stage. (Witness the banning of Nick Hanauer's TED talk on income inequality and taxing the rich, albeit disputed by TED as an instance of censorship.)[30] This lack of diversity is perhaps captured best in the rapt audiences present in every video, who are visibly homogeneous—and united in their ability to pay at least $7,500 (2012 prices) for a seat. For access to speaker receptions, which is bundled in 'Patron Status', the cost skyrockets to $125,000.[31]

KHAN ACADEMY

In many ways, Khan Academy is *the* paradigmatic Open Education platform. The Academy came out of hedge fund manager Sal Khan's attempts, in 2004, to find long-distance, visual means by which to teach his cousin elements of mathematics she was having trouble with. These efforts were then systematised as more and more friends and family sought to share his lessons. The organisation was formally incorporated as late as 2008, and in 2009 Khan left his hedge fund job to dedicate himself full time to the venture. In 2010, Khan Academy received its first large grants from Google ($2 million), and the Bill and Melinda Gates Foundation ($1.5 million). Presently, the site features thousands of self-created videos: science, math, and technology lessons predominate, but the Academy has made an alliance to broaden this to the arts and humanities, namely through incorporation of 'SmartHistory', which specialises in this area.[32]

Khan Academy however has an educational philosophy centred on the kind of individualised, self-determined learning whose centrality within the commercialised version of Open Education is (as illustrated by the move from cMOOCs to xMOOCs) not a necessary or 'natural' feature. (In fact, we will go on to argue quite the opposite: that education—and Open Education with it—should be regarded as a distinctly social, and socialising, activity.) Here, achievement drives progress—in that one only moves on when one has mastered a subject—and there is an intense culture of self-assessment and monitoring built into Khan Academy's systems. These include features like the 'knowledge map',[33] where the total knowledge available on the platform is mapped out, and challenges are suggested to master it. Khan Academy shares this and other 'systems feedback' features—analysing patterns across data sets and behaviours—with MIT/Harvard's edX project, which describes one of its primary aims as to understand 'how learning happens'. (As argued in several instances in this study, it may be this kind of data on user activity—or its analysis—which might ultimately provide the 'value', or marketable object, that parent companies are seeking to capture on these platforms, generating what we, in our educational context chapter, described as their 'ulterior motive' for engaging in Open Education activity).

WIKIVERSITY

The Wikipedia Foundation is the non-profit umbrella organisation supporting the vast array of open access knowledge repositories and collaborative platforms residing under the Wikipedia name (for example, Wikitionary, Wikiquote, Wikibooks, Wikisource, Wikimedia Commons, Wikispecies, Wikinews, Wikiversity, Wikimedia Incubator and Meta-Wiki). The foundation operates along open organisation principles and is based in the tech-hub 'Market' area of San Francisco, where its generous support from the Valley's digerati grants it deep pockets. The Wikipedia Foundation's income for 2011 exceeded $25 million.

The Wikipedia Foundation's contributor base of 60,000 derives primarily from the Wikipedia project. In light of this enormous number, the enigma of Wikiversity—the foundation's educational initiative—has been its failure to gain momentum. After running for over six years, the English language version has only a few hundred active users out of half a million registrations. Even an outreach initiative put in place in 2010 by Wikipedia's CEO, Sue Gardner, which was supported by a $1.2 million grant from the Stanton Foundation and enabled Wikipedians to provide training in its methodologies to students and teachers, still hasn't been able to affect a change. Sue Gardner and the governing board have attempted to address this in successive policy reviews but with little effect.

There are so many lessons to take home from the Wikipedia Foundation's very public experiment that it would be an injustice to attempt to sum them up. Instead, we will offer one observation based on attempts to bring the U.K. Wikipedia chapters together with U.K. cultural organisations, which some of us started doing as part of Wikipedia's GLAM-Wiki programme (for Galleries Libraries Archives and Museums).[34] In a way, the excessively technical nature of its projects run counter to Wikipedia Foundation's aims for audience inclusion and diversity. Quite simply, to have any chance of contributing to Wikipedia you must have high technical or writing skills. Consensus among the Wikipedia community is that this ensures a quality filter, preventing erroneous or malicious posts. But another, equally important effect is for a set of pre-engineered goals and values to be reproduced, and for the hoped-for diversity in Wikipedia's contributor community—which in turn has dramatic effects on its notionally objective 'informational' content—to be precluded. (The latter has recently been illustrated very forcefully in the global Art and Feminism Wikithon. This event tackled what it described as Wikipedia's historical 'gender trouble' (a lower than 13 per cent female quotient in editors) by organising a day-long editing and inputting session on female artists.)[35]

CODECADEMY

Codecademy represents a new category of Open Education provider using the free provision of skills training online to achieve something different than advertised. It offers a fresh example of how new variants of Open Education are lending themselves to a burgeoning range of business models and policy objectives.

Based in New York with—at the time of writing—over $12 million of investment, Codecademy offers free online training in a variety of relatively accessible web programming areas such as HTML5, Java and CSS. Codecademy is infused with a transformational zeal that is typical of this business 'space'. A representative company slogan: 'Education is broken. Come help us build the education the world deserves'.[36] Its courses can be quite involved, running from hours to days. Yet when companies like this boast of having a million plus site users, they refrain from mentioning that, instead of education, or training provision, the business model behind their free learning offer is actually based on helping companies with their employee recruitment, for which they can earn a substantial fee (passing on details of potential recruits earns on average 20 per cent of eighteen months' worth of salary won).

SELF-ORGANISED I: 'INFORMAL' LIBRARIES

Despite their radical approach to openness, these niche services—currently the most well known (if that is the right term to use in this context) are aaaaarg.org and libgen.info, formerly Gigapedia and library .nu—remain remarkably opaque. They typically cultivate an aura of obscurity and exclusivity, in part out of necessity. A lot of their content is illegally obtained, so maintainers are obscure or even anonymous out of fear of legal liability or of being taken down by their hosting services. The participating 'communities' tend to be similarly opaque. Many of these sites survive by avoiding overly mainstream content, 'rich' media, and a consistent level of quality that might provoke rights-holders. (Given the platforms' liminal status, it is widely thought that rights-holders are more likely to weigh informal promotional potential against perceived lost revenues, though obviously Gigapedia and aaaaarg.org have been exceptions in being forced either to come offline or endlessly change names/domains.)[37] These sites' strategies— if they can be called that—have pros and cons. For example, the fact that content is user-contributed tends to assure materials are responsive to particular communities of interest. However, the selections can be arbitrary and eclectic, and formats unpredictable (poor-quality PDFs, high-quality OCRs, error-ridden EPUBs/MOBIs and so on). Related strategies involve various forms of gatekeeping, both active and passive. Active strategies can include requiring an invitation from a known user or requiring users to maintain some ratio of uploads to downloads. Passive strategies can take the form of denying access to search spiders and providing only rudimentary internal search functions (by author or title). Such strategies may deter enforcement, but they also severely restrict utility by making direct links from other sites impossible. As a result, these informal libraries are often best understood in the way they are used—as repositories (rather than online self-learning spaces). However, their transience further limits their utility even in this regard, because links to the homepage tend to 'rot'.

SELF-ORGANISED II: THE PUBLIC SCHOOL

The Public School (TPS) is a self-learning initiative which represents many of the qualities of a subset of Open Education that we might categorise as 'grassroots' but which has, in fact, never affiliated itself with the concept (similar projects being London Occupy's Tent City University and others, as mentioned in chapter 1).[38] As described above, the pedagogical turn in art, too, has provided many examples, as documented recently in *Frieze* magazine's feature on 'new schools', which included a statement from The Public School, among coverage of SOMA, Mexico City; Islington Mill Academy, Salford; MASS Alexandria, in Egypt; and The Silent University and School of Global Art, London.[39] The Public School's discourse of self-organisation synchronises with the critique issuing from within the student struggle and other places regarding the instrumental role played by HEIs within the knowledge economy, whilst simultaneously providing a concrete alternative to their mass industrialised model of education (the 'edu-factory'). Although it is unique in systematising and describing it, The Public School shares with other initiatives a relatively horizontal decision-making structure, where, what one might—echoing traditional HEIs—call 'learning aims' (the reading of a book or a text, or the collective engagement with a particular subject) are set collaboratively and through web-based decision-making tools/structures. The latter are carefully managed so that executive power is monitored, rotated, etc.

Given this is an independent, minimally subsidised venture, the clear functionality and apparent efficiency of its systems—as compared to much larger projects attempting similar things—is striking. Its experiments with global franchising models, while problematic for some, are also noteworthy. There are, for example, attempts to create both 'universal' (as in universally shared) and 'localised' (as in particular to specific franchise locations) educational programmes, that aim to lend the project as a whole global relevance and a modicum of unity, while simultaneously avoiding the kind of standardisation that assumes a universality in social, economic and cultural contexts. Franchises in Berlin, Brussels, Durham, Chicago, Helsinki, New York, Los Angeles and San Juan would seem to indicate that there is enthusiasm for this model. It will come as no surprise that The Public School is resolutely opposed to accreditation of any kind. It celebrates learning as part of life, and knowledge as an unquantifiable good.

NOTES

1. 'When Ideals Meet Reality', Jisc Infastructure Team, http://infteam.jisc involve.org/wp/2012/09/25/ideals_reality/.

2. See http://www.jisc.ac.uk.

3. See http://www.theodi.org/. In the United States there are constraints on such state activities (a state of affairs which hopefully will not be replicated in the United Kingdom). At their most extreme, these constraints can stipulate that public domain data must not disadvantage private sector interests—meaning that, if a subsidised university library wanted to provide services to the public cheaper than a commercial provider this would be prohibited. (Instead, universities would have to buy free public data back at a price!) There are major problems associated with an opening up of public data, to be sure, but this is not one of them.

4. Wellcome Trust, 'Wellcome Trust Strengthens Its Open Access Policy', *Wellcome Trust*, June 28, 2012, http://www.wellcome.ac.uk/News/Media -office/Press-releases/2012/WTVM055745.htm.

5. John Holmwood, 'Commercial Enclosure: Whatever Happened to Open Access?', *Radical Philosophy*, 181, Sept/Oct. 2013, http://www.radicalphilosophy .com/commentary/commercial-enclosure.

6. See Walter Russell Mead, 'The Higher Ed Bubble Is Very, Very Real', *The American Interest*, December 21, 2012, http://blogs.the-american-interest .com/wrm/2012/12/21/the-higher-ed-bubble-is-very-very-real/#sthash.N6 EvCeM1.dpuf. For a more sceptical view, see R.A., 'Is Higher Education a Bubble?', *The Economist*, May 13, 2011, http://www.economist.com/blogs/freeex change/2011/05/education.

7. Christopher F. Schuetze, 'Europe's Budget Crisis Hits Universities', *New York Times*, November 25, 2012, http://www.nytimes.com/2012/11/26/world/europe/europes-budget-crisis-hits-universities.html?pagewanted=all.

8. See, for example, Nicole Allen, 'Open Textbooks and Solving the College Cost Crisis', Beyond Content: Open Education Conference, Vancouver, British Columbia, Oct. 16–18, 2012, http://openedconference.org/2012/program/archive-of-sessions/day-2/day2-1330-c400/.

9. For example, the Provincial Government of British Columbia announced a free digital textbook programme at the Beyond Content: Open Education Conference. See http://www2.news.gov.bc.ca/news_releases_2009-2013/2012AEIT0010-001581.htm.

10. Sna Sna, 'How New Startup Knewton Will Solve the Global Education Crisis', *PolicyMic*, February 10, 2012, http://www.policymic.com/articles/4084/how-new-startup-knewton-will-solve-the-global-education-crisis; http://2u.com/about/; Tamar Lewin, 'Online Enterprises Gain Foothold as Path to a College Degree', *New York Times*, August 25, 2011, http://www.nytimes.com/2011/08/25/education/25future.html.

11. It should be noted that Knewton is not 'open'.

12. As of the time of writing (June 2014) FutureLearn has thirty-eight partners, including many Russell Group universities—although there are some notable absences from that list.

13. For an account of an American defensive response, see Ry Rivard, 'Duke Faculty Say No', *Inside Higher Education*, April 30, 2013, http://www.insidehighered.com/news/2013/04/30/duke-faculty-reject-plan-it-join-online-consortium.

14. See http://www.globalnxt.edu.my/about/university-of-the-future-model and http://www.globalnxt.edu.my/about/university-partnerships. While carrying the legacy of the Universitas 21 Global consortium project, this 'global university' should not be confused with its namesake, Universitas 21, a comparable network of international research universities which is very much operational and can be found at http://www.universitas21.com.

15. As one of the few non-profits in this section, Peer to Peer University (P2PU) illustrates another of the Open Education types we have discussed in this chapter, namely the notionally philanthropic agency with an eye on the global economic, regulatory, and internet environment (backed, as we have described, by funders like the William and Flora Hewlett Foundation or, as here, the South Africa–based Shuttleworth Foundation). See http://info.p2pu.org/about/ and Katherine Mangan, 'In This Online University, Students Do the Teaching as Well as the Learning', *Chronicle of Higher Education*, June 18, 2012, http://chronicle.com/article/In-This-Online-University/132307/.

16. It is current U.K. government strategy to change this by inviting and favouring private sector investment.

17. John Daniel, 'Making Sense of MOOCs: Musing in a Maze of Myth, Paradox and Possibility', 2012, http://academicpartnerships.com/docs/default -document-library/moocs.pdf?sfvrsn=0.

18. See, for example, the previously mentioned series of working papers on MOOCs recently made available by Harvard University (http:// harvardx.harvard.edu/harvardx-working-papers) and MIT (http://odl.mit.edu/ mitx-working-papers/).

19. Sean Coughlan, 'Harvard Plans to Boldly Go with "Spocs"', BBC News: Business, September 24, 2013, http://www.bbc.co.uk/news/business-24166247.

20. On this note, the emergence of the new phenomenon (and acronym) 'SPOCs' for Small Private Online Courses is telling, responding as it does to the perceived failure of MOOCs to gain traction. See Tim Goral, 'SPOCs May Provide What MOOCs Can't', *University Business*, July 2013, http://www.uni versitybusiness.com/article/spocs-may-provide-what-moocs-can't.

21. *Universities UK, Massive Open Online Courses: Higher Education's Digital Moment?* (London: Universities UK, 2013), http://www.universitiesuk .ac.uk/highereducation/Documents/2013/MassiveOpenOnlineCourses.pdf.

22. 'Penn GSE Study Shows MOOCs Have Relatively Few Active Users, with Only a Few Persisting to Course End', *Press Room*, December 5, 2013, http://www.gse.upenn.edu/pressroom/press-releases/2013/12/penn-gse-study -shows-moocs-have-relatively-few-active-users-only-few-persisti.

23. See 'Data Mining Exposes Embarrassing Problems for Massive Open Online Courses', *MIT Technology Review*, December 18, 2013, http://www .technologyreview.com/view/522816/data-mining-exposes-embarrassing -problems-for-massive-open-online-courses/.

24. Another recent study from the University of Pennsylvania supports what many have already observed about MOOCs (that is, that most students are male and already possess a traditional university degree), finding that the student population for one of its Coursera MOOCS tends to be 'young, well educated, and employed, with a majority from developed countries' (Gayle Christensen, Andrew Steinmetz, Brandon Alcorn, Amy Bennett, Deirdre Woods, and Ezekiel J. Emanuel, *The MOOC Phenomenon: Who Takes Massive Open Online Courses and Why?* [November 6, 2013], http://papers.ssrn.com/ sol3/papers.cfm?abstract_id=2350964).

25. For criticism of this phenomenon, see Tressie McMillan Cottom, 'The Audacity: Thrun Learns a Lesson and Students Pay', *Tressiemc*, November 19, 2013, http://tressiemc.com/2013/11/19/the-audacity-thrun-learns-a-lesson -and-students-pay/.

26. Tamar Lewin, 'Instruction for Masses Knocks Down Campus Walls', *New York Times*, March 4, 2012, http://www.nytimes.com/2012/03/05/education/ moocs-large-courses-open-to-all-topple-campus-walls.html?pagewanted=all.

27. See ALTO UK, *Jisc*, http://www.jisc.ac.uk/whatwedo/programmes/ ukoer3/altouk.aspx.

28. Bernard Stiegler, 'Bernard Stiegler, director of IRI (Innovation and Research Institute) at the Georges Pompidou Centre, and WWW2012 keynote speaker', *21st International World Wide Web Conference*, Lyon, France, April 16–20, 2012, http://www2012.wwwconference.org/hidden/interview-of-bernard-stiegler/.

29. Chris Anderson, 'TED and Inequality: The Real Story', *TEDChris: The Untweetable*, May 17, 2012, http://archive.is/qdHfa.

30. Nick Hanauer, 'A TED Talk on Income Inequality', May 17, 2012, http://www.youtube.com/watch?v=ilhOXCgSunc.

31. See http://www.ted.com/pages/tedconferences_attend#levelsofmembership. For critical engagements with TED which are even more scathing, see Evgeny Morozov, 'The Naked and the TED', *The New Republic*, August 2, 2012, http://www.tnr.com/article/books-and-arts/magazine/105703/the-naked-and-the-ted-khanna#; Thomas Frank, 'TED Talks Are Lying to You', *Salon*, October 13, 2013, http://www.salon.com/2013/10/13/ted_talks_are_lying_to_you/; and Benjamin H. Bratton, 'We Need to Talk About TED', *Bratton.info*, December 2013, http://www.bratton.info/projects/talks/we-need-to-talk-about-ted/.

32. See http://khan.smarthistory.org.

33. See http://www.khanacademy.org/exercisedashboard.

34. This effort was part of a larger digital strategy project for London-based cultural organisations organised by Mute Publishing's digital agency, Open-Mute, under the title 'Art of Digital London' (2009–2012).

35. See http://en.wikipedia.org/wiki/Wikipedia:Meetup/ArtAndFeminism.

36. Codecademy's 'About Us' section, too, is a defiant summary of a particularly aggressive variant of Open Education. It claims not merely to 'disrupt' education (as it says other companies do) but to *rethink* it 'from the ground up' in order to create a first truly 'net native' incarnation—which takes its cues from Zynga and Facebook rather than the classroom. See http://www.codecademy.com/about.

37. For a discussion of an exception to this general attitude on the part of rights-holders, as represented by the self-professed 'radical publishing house' Verso Books, see Hall, 'Pirate Radical Philosophy'.

38. The Public School can be found at http://www.thepublicschool.org. Its differentiation from Open Education is well captured in its strapline, which states: 'The Public School is a school with no curriculum. It is not accredited, it does not give out degrees, and it has no affiliation with the public school system. It is a framework that supports autodidactic activities, operating under the assumption that everything is in everything'.

39. See 'New Schools', *Frieze* 149 (September 2012), http://www.frieze.com/issue/article/new-schools/, and Sean Dockray, 'For an External Programme', *The Public School*, November 12, 2012, http://thepublicschool.org/node/31842. The latter text also functions as an excellent summary of the Public School's view on the phenomenon of Open Education, particularly as embodied in a project like the MIT–Harvard collaboration edX (https://www.edx.org/about-us).

6

❖ ❖

Towards a Philosophy
of Open Education

In this study of Open Education we have attempted to problematise the notion that the worldwide population will be the primary beneficiary of a move towards technologically enhanced learning. In fact, we have been at pains to argue that a significant amount of Open Education activity is only very subtly different from its supposed opposite—traditional, 'closed' learning—in comparison to which it may not offer exactly the *same* problems (cost, access, distribution, quality), just new and marginally different ones. To boot, Open Education is likely to be used strategically in arguments for the disinvestment in the 'bricks and mortar' of single, historically and culturally distinct universities. Having said that, the unprecedented pace at which these two categories of learning are hybridising probably makes a binary separation or even comparison counterproductive.

RECOMPOSING THE UNIVERSITY

As higher education faces rapidly escalating pressure to redefine itself, the net effect is a demand to 'unbundle' traditional approaches to disciplines and institutional constructions. At introductory levels (and especially in U.S. institutions) where more general curricula predominate, these reformulations are more easily accomplished, because the main 'markets' for their 'product', as it were, are internal—elective departments and programmes. However, at more advanced levels the impact of unbundling may be much more severe—and success more likely to be defined in terms of, and measured by, external markets (graduates' work placement, destination data, assessments of research excellence and so on). Moreover, these internal segmentations often correlate with faculty rank and promotion issues, which are heavily shaped by familiar divides between, for example, 'teaching' and 'research'. Thus Open Education's potential will often be similarly segmented within the institution, with varying degrees of relevance and focus. To risk a dramatic oversimplification, at lower levels (for example, early career scholars and researchers), it is possible that the impact of Open Education will centre on pedagogy and curricula, whereas at higher levels (for example, university professors) it is more likely to affect research and publishing. (This is the case, not just because their seniority means university professors may be more heavily involved with research than teaching, but also because they are often in a better position to be able to take any perceived risk in adopting the philosophies, strategies and techniques of Open Education with regard to their research.) Even if an institution manages to effectively disseminate its findings on an Open Educational Resource and open access basis, the range of issues addressed—from more or less generalisable pedagogical and curricular techniques to substantive material within an highly specialised field of research—might be disparate (that is, the more specialist, hard-won, 'original', credit-worthy and valuable the material is perceived to be, the more proprietary feelings it is possible it may evoke—say, if there is the potential for it to form the basis of a spin-off company).

From a systemic viewpoint, these kinds of issues may well fall within the ambient level of organisational 'noise'—changes in HR practices regarding staff development and promotion, shifting *foci* of recruitment and placement, revisions to university mission statements, trends within various fields and so on. In keeping with the view, articulated in our preface, of higher learning as an extremely complex field defined by contending constituencies, each case and area will need to be carefully analysed and addressed in its specificity. Still, as regards provision in our own areas of media and cultural studies, we feel certain tentative conclusions can legitimately be drawn:

- The arts and humanities are either absent or lagging far behind STEM subjects in Open Education environments.
- Within what does exist of the arts and humanities, the field of media and cultural studies is relatively invisible. (For one interesting example, however, see FemTechNet's DOCC [Distributed Open Collaborative Course].)[1] Better represented are history, art history and English literature—as these are possibly seen as easier to 'deliver' online; and are also perhaps less critical in their approach to both the idea of the university, and to digital media, than certain areas of media and cultural studies (see our section Media and Cultural Studies PLC in chapter 7 for more).

Of course joining the Open Education bandwagon is hard to resist if everyone else is doing so. No one wants to be left behind. As Ian Bogost remarks regarding the July 2012 announcement by his university, Georgia Tech, and eleven other HEIs of their decision to participate in Coursera, 'institutions like mine are afraid of the present and the future yet drunk on the dream of being "elite" and willing to do anything to be seen in the right crowd making the hip choices.'[2] Nevertheless, our argument here is that, given the present market fervour around Open Education, attempting to simply add to the currently available Open Education offerings with an arts and humanities- or media and cultural studies-flavoured MOOC is not *necessarily* particularly helpful. Indeed, it seems to us that what is really lacking is not so much another instance of Open Education, but rather a careful, rigorous, critical engagement with the Open Education phenomenon as it is now taking shape.

TRADITIONAL LIBERAL EDUCATION AS ELITE PRESERVE?

For us, an intellectually responsible approach to Open Education would engage much more critically with its own developmental processes. After all, in the five years since Geser and Atkins et al. produced their influential reports on Open Educational Resources, the coherent, systematic planning and funding of OERs that they assess (and also typify) has made way for a sort of Wild West of public-private partnerships, PR ruses and telecoms competitions, which shake and trouble the central terms of reference almost to the point of meaninglessness.[3] Here, as we have said, Open Education clearly has a role to play in the creation of a supposedly more flexible, efficient, economically instrumental and cost-effective two-tier university system. This is a system whereby traditional 'liberal educational ideals like meritocratic access, face-to-face learning, and the disinterested pursuit of knowledge' become the 'elite preserve of those able to pay top dollar for such handcrafted attention';[4] while those who can't pay, or can't pay so much, or belong to those groups who prefer not to move away to university (lower-income families, recent immigrant families, orthodox religious groups), have to make do with a poor, online, distance, and self-learning second-rate alternative produced by a reduced number of global corporations (the business model of a whole middle tier of universities having been creatively disrupted and displaced). And as Carole Leathwood, Professor of Education at the Institute for Policy Studies in Education, London Metropolitan University, points out:

> The elite universities are already able to spend considerably more per student on things such as libraries, computing facilities, sports and careers advice. . . . The pattern of wealthier students going to wealthier universities and poorer students going to the financially less well-off institutions is already established.
>
> Research shows that working class, women and some minority ethnic groups tend to be more debt averse than their white middle class peers, and that financial considerations strongly impact upon decisions of which university to attend—particularly for working class students.[5]

Open Education is something the arts and humanities in general, and media and cultural studies in particular, should certainly take seriously and have a strong interest in. As Mark C. Taylor makes clear:

> It is correctly argued that education at every level should be the right of all and not the privilege of a few. In the absence of increased funding for financial aid, it will be necessary to undertake new institutional initiatives to expand educational opportunities without significantly increasing costs.[6]

Open Education offers at least one possibility for undertaking such initiatives. In the process it provides a potential means of responding to the direction in which the English HE system is heading after the

Brown report of 2010.[7] It is a direction in which it is increasingly only the children of the upper and middle classes who will be able to afford to attend a traditional university given that, even before the raising of tuition fees in 2012, the U.K. was in a situation where 'young people from middle class backgrounds are more than twice as likely to participate in higher education as their working-class peers'.[8]

But Open Education also offers a means of responding to the emphasis of the U.K. government on STEM and on instrumental, applied research that can demonstrate an impact on society and the economy (and this despite the fact that, according to recent figures from the U.K. government's own Department for Culture, Media & Sport, the creative industries 'are worth more than £36 billion a year; they generate £70,000 every minute for the UK economy; and they employ 1.5 million people'.)[9] Open Education could help us to continue to conduct arts and humanities-orientated learning, teaching and research in a context where the amount of financial and institutional support the arts and humanities receive has been significantly reduced. Indeed, many fear it may soon only be a few privileged—some would call them traditional and conservative—universities that will be able to afford to conduct arts and humanities teaching and research.[10] They cite as evidence the 2011 launch of the New College of the Humanities in London by the liberal philosopher A. C. Grayling.[11] A non-profit subsidiary of the for-profit Tertiary Education Services, this is a private, 'Oxbridge-style' institution offering undergraduate degrees in English, history, philosophy, classical studies and history of art—but not of course media and cultural studies—taught by academic 'stars' such as Richard Dawkins and Steven Pinker for £18,000 a year, £54,000 over the three years of an undergraduate degree.

OPEN EDUCATION: IN THEORY AND IN PRACTICE

The challenge as we see it is to invent and institute approaches to Open Education that are pragmatic yet *critical*, ambitious about their visibility yet *creative* and *experimental*, willing to take risks and be surprising—not least by keeping open the question of what Open Education actually is and can be. Accordingly, these approaches would not adhere to the absolutism of utopian-affirmative Open Education discourses (whose unspoken but clearly latent tendency, particularly at a time of global financial crisis and public resource cuts, is often towards a disruption of existing higher education infrastructures in favour of 'efficient', flexible, instrumental, commercial providers—witness the recent warning from the U.K. government that employers unhappy with the skill-set of university leavers could set up their own MOOCs to assess the abilities of potential employees, only interviewing those who have successfully completed the course).[12] But neither would they engage in the kind of critical theoretical project that would disallow or denigrate (or be in any simple sense contrasted or otherwise opposed to) pragmatic engagement with the 'lived' manifestations of the phenomenon itself (tools, institutions, communities). Instead, the educational mission would be to nurture 'critical open education' along with a practice of positive, experimental, transformative engagement.

Although it should not be taken as a definitive or final list, we propose the following speculative principles for such a practice:

- **Explicitly frame Open Education as social and socialising.** Fields such as media studies, radical pedagogy, the digital humanities and education-oriented art practice have already done a certain amount of thinking about the changing role of educators in a networked environment. This work should be built on and radicalised further. In particular, and as a strategic corrective to much of what currently goes under the banner of Open Education, the primacy of group work and social activity should be brought to the fore in projects; individualised consumption of Open Education (as described in Khan Academy, for example) should *not* replace an understanding of learning as an inherently social, discursive and relational activity, that has the capacity to build 'communities of learning' that stretch across time and space—and also institutions.
- **Find ways of connecting with other movements dealing with issues of openness**: not just those associated with open access, open data, open science, grey literature, altmetrics and so on, but also the digital humanities, FLOSS, p2p networks, the pro-piracy movement and grey commons.
- **Collaborate with international partners.** A rigorous critical approach to Open Education could foster what might be called a

'bi-directional' stance, by consistently querying what provision from the west or global north to other regions means for the educational experience being offered. While the imperialist undertones are not always easy to demonstrate in the first category of subjects coming online, the political problems inherent in American Ivy League and British Russell Group universities 'educating the world' are hard to ignore. (As John Daniel notes: 'Already, at the 2009 UNESCO World Conference on Higher Education, the president of the 300,000-student University of South Africa [UNISA] labelled Open Educational Resources as a form of intellectual neo-colonialism'.)[13] In this respect, finding international partners that are similarly disposed towards—and can help to provide—multipolar analyses of, and engagement with, the Open Education phenomenon would be invaluable to any critical approach.

- **Experiment with sound and vision** (at the very least). Responses to Open Education materials show that those with the most interesting and profound effect often have a unique, 'medium-specific' quality over and above the direct relay of 'talking heads'. As mentioned before (in our section on MOOCs), students cite the ability to play back, consider, and watch up close as determining factors for interest in Open Education, all of which can be accentuated by intelligent visual design. Together with a strong emphasis on media 'literacy' (if that is not too grammatological a term for it), an inventive and experimental approach to Open Education could thus draw on and develop expertise in graphic and video production (to take just two of many possible examples) to critically explore Open Education materials as a media form possessing a certain singularity.
- **Avoid monolithic systems.** This recommendation pertains both to the technical platforms HEIs provide, and inclusion of Web 2.0 and social media in Acceptable Use Policies. As well as adopting a self-conscious and self-reflexive attitude towards such platforms, a careful, rigorous Open Education should be ready for sudden technological changes in the education sector and outside it, and use strategic partnerships actively to build this preparedness.
- **Learn from agile and rapid development methodologies.** These could be employed when bringing together the intersecting areas of legal, technical and economic practice that need to play a part in innovation in Open Education. An example framework is the

Dynamic Systems Development Method (DSDM) Consortium, which has an academic programme.[14]

- **Understand and use co-creation.** Dealt with judiciously (that is, without engaging in surveillance activity!), co-creation, data analysis/mining, and 'radical metrics', coupled with 'distributed storytelling' media planning strategies, could also be used by any approach to Open Education willing to take risks and be surprising, not least to increase student engagement.[15]

- **Produce more comprehensive analysis of media and cultural studies-related Open Education provision in the United Kingdom/Europe.** In line with our principle that any rigorous, critical Open Education be positioned more clearly and self-consciously, all the above will benefit from ongoing study of other courses being provided in areas such as digital humanities, science and technology studies, digital and data journalism, media arts, etc.

- **Engage critically.** We see a rigorous and inventive media and cultural studies in part as having the potential to fulfil this function, drawing on its existing expertise in the critique of, and engagement with, media (now integrating itself ever more deeply into higher education). The distortion of the Open Education field that has occurred as a result of the powerful marketing and PR of the predominantly affirmative approach of players currently determining the game (elite universities, private tech companies, venture capital–backed initiatives) means that such a careful critical engagement—one that draws in legal, technical, economic and philosophical issues—could make an important and much-needed contribution to a broader strategy for proactive experimentation with new and emerging 'open education', designed to generate possibilities for a radically different model of the university from those with which we are familiar. And not only that, but a radically different kind of economy and way of organising post-industrial society too—one that could start with us and our own politico-institutional practices as university workers; an economy and way of organising society based more on openness, responsibility and a theory of the gift, for example, and far less on possession, acquisition, accumulation, competition, celebrity, and ideas of academic work and labour as something to be owned and commodified as the property of individuals.[16]

Here again (as in our preface), the last assumption should be regarded as governing all others. We see it as constituting an attempt on our part to encourage the taking of rigorous and responsible (Chantal Mouffe follows Jacques Derrida in calling them undecidable) political and ethical decisions (or what Karen Barad thinks of in terms of *cuts*) with regard to Open Education;[17] and in the process bring into question many of the ideas Open Education projects tend to take for granted: ideas of the author, authority, subjectivity, originality, the work, the book, fixity, piracy, the law, copyright, and so on.

FREE LABOUR

To provide a brief example of the kind of decisions that could be taken, let us address a complaint often raised against Open Education: that, in many of its guises, it is involved in 'encouraging' people—a good number of whom are already overworked and underpaid—to work for free. While this is undeniably true ('Georgia Tech's Coursera faculty are taking on the task on top of their normal work', Bogost notes),[18] there are three points we would raise by way of response that might mitigate in favour of taking a decision to become involved in Open Education nonetheless:

- Academics, thinkers, researchers and scholars in privileged positions and working at relatively wealthy institutions have time bought for them in the shape of lighter teaching loads, research and teaching assistants, sabbaticals, and other forms of support for their teaching, research and administrative responsibilities. Yet time—to conduct research, to write and to publish, to keep up with the field, even to just think and reflect—is what many of those in less privileged positions and working at less wealthy institutions do not have. So it is important that those who are in a position to do so give something back by *gifting* at least a portion of their time to trying to change this situation by supporting others with their teaching, learning and research, in some form at least. What is more, it is important to do so now more than ever. Due to changes in the economy, and the crisis in funding detailed above, ours may be the last generation with the full-time posts

that provide *some* time free from arduous working conditions and
heavily loaded teaching timetables.[19]

- Even in a context where interested academics and researchers
are willing and able to devote a portion of their time to trying to
change this situation by becoming involved with Open Education,
this would not *necessarily* require them to donate *additional* free
labour. Of course, establishing an academic equivalent to The 1
Per Cent campaign initiated in 2005 by Public Architecture might
be an interesting and important thing to do:

> The 1% program of Public Architecture connects nonprofit organiza-
> tions in need of design assistance with architecture and design firms
> willing to donate their time on a pro bono basis. . . . If every architec-
> ture professional in the U.S. committed 1% of their time to pro bono
> service, it would add up to 5,000,000 hours annually—the equivalent of
> a 2,500-person firm, working full-time for the public good.[20]

However, contributing to Open Education projects need not
require academics to take on additional work. After all, they
already donate a large amount of free labour to publishers and
journals in the form of writing, peer-reviewing and other forms
of editorial activity. According to one estimate, calculated using
the Peer Review Survey 2009, when it comes to the 1.3 million
peer-reviewed journals that are published annually, academics
donate the equivalent of £200 million a year of their time to peer-
reviewing alone.[21] Any academics interested in getting involved
with Open Education could therefore simply stop giving their
free labour to journals and publishers who do not allow authors,
as a bare minimum, to self-archive the refereed and accepted
final drafts of their publications in open access repositories; or
that are owned by multinational for-profit corporations involved,
say, with the military or arms trade;[22] or that aggressively avoid
paying the standard rate of corporation tax in the United Kingdom,[23] and devote that time and energy to working on an Open
Education basis instead.

In doing so they would be joining forces with the many academics who have already taken a stand on such issues. As early as
2002 Ted Bergstrom, Chair of Economics at the University of California Santa Barbara, declared he was going to fight back against

journals he believed to be using monopolisation to overcharge institutional libraries by refusing to referee papers for those that operate annual library subscription charges of $1,000 or more, in favour of journals which charge less than $300.[24]

Bergstrom was followed in 2007 by Nick Montfort, an Associate Professor of Digital Media at MIT, who stated he was no longer prepared to review articles for non-public, non–open access, for-profit journals.[25] Similarly in 2008 danah boyd, a Fellow at the Harvard Berkman Center for Internet and Society, publically vowed that her article 'Facebook's Privacy Trainwreck: Exposure, Invasion, and Social Convergence', which appeared in a 2008 special issue of the Sage journal *Convergence*, edited by Henry Jenkins and Mark Deuze, would be the last she was prepared to 'publish to which the public cannot get access. I am boycotting locked-down journals and I'd like to ask other academics to do the same'.[26] By 2012, Harvard University was itself advocating that its faculty should make their research available open access by submitting it to open access journals and repositories, and that they should even consider resigning from publications that insist on keeping access to research toll access only.[27] The entire editorial board of one journal, the *Journal of Library Administration*, did exactly that in protest at the restrictive licensing terms of the author agreement of its publisher, Taylor & Francis.[28]

• The system whereby we have a whole host of underpaid graduates carrying out a significant amount of university teaching and marking, but only having part-time or temporary contracts, with little job security or long-term prospects, is something the current academic economy has produced.[29] It is this system, in which academic labour is proletarianised and rendered exploitative, tedious, repetitive and mundane, that Open Education could potentially act against by helping to create opportunities for *work* rather than mere *employment*, for teaching and research as a labour of love rather than as a mere job.[30] For instance, it is not difficult to envisage a critical Open Education project offering a means of making responsible decisions or cuts designed precisely to counter the *becoming business* of the university—not least by providing academics and researchers with an opportunity to also *say no* to the contemporary neoliberal institution's culture of bureaucracy, audits and managerialist control through the strategic withdrawal of (at least some of) their labour and donation of it elsewhere. Mark Fisher has engaged with this problematic to suggest:

> If neoliberalism triumphed by incorporating the desires of the post 68 working class, a new left could begin by building on the desires which neoliberalism has generated but which it has been unable to satisfy. For example, the left should argue that it can deliver what neoliberalism signally failed to do: a massive reduction of bureaucracy. What is needed is a new struggle over work and who controls it; an assertion of worker autonomy (as opposed to control by management) together with a rejection of certain kinds of labor (such as the excessive auditing which has become so central [a] feature of work in post-Fordism) . . . New forms of industrial action need to be instituted against managerialism. For instance, in the case of teachers and lecturers, the tactic of strikes (or even marking bans) should be abandoned, because they only hurt students and members. . . . What is needed is the strategic withdrawal of forms of labor which will only be noticed by management: all of the machineries of self-surveillance that have no effect whatsoever on the delivery of education, but which managerialism could not exist without.[31]

CREATIVE COMMONS CRITIQUE

When it comes to the kind of ideas Open Education projects tend to take for granted, an experimental, inventive, pragmatic, yet critical approach to Open Education could, for example, interrogate the use of Creative Commons licenses by the P2P university and other Open Education and Open Educational Resources projects (including our own—see chapter 7), on the grounds that what these licenses offer is a reform of intellectual property, not a fundamental critique of it.[32] In fact, Creative Commons's *whole notion of the Commons* has already been subjected to a certain amount of critique on the basis that:

- The concern of Creative Commons is with reserving rights of copyright owners rather than granting them to users.
- Creative Commons is extremely liberal and individualistic, offering authors a range of licences from which they can individually

choose rather than promoting a collective agreement, policy or philosophy.

• What Creative Commons actually offers is a reform of IP, not a fundamental critique of, or challenge to, IP.[33]

From this perspective, Creative Commons is not actually advocating a *common* stock of non-owned creative works that everyone is free to use at all. On the contrary, it presumes that everything created by an author or artist is *their property*. If anything, Creative Commons is concerned with helping the law to adapt to the new conditions created by digital culture by 'promoting a more flexible model of private ownership'.[34] Creative Commons's emphasis on the rights of copyright owners can be seen to function strategically, as it holds strong appeal to what Andrew Ross describes as 'the thwarted class fraction of high-skilled and self-directed individuals in the creative and knowledge sectors whose entrepreneurial prospects are increasingly blocked by corporate monopolies.'[35] Proponents of this view of IP have thus been able to form a 'coalition of experts with the legal access and resources'—Lawrence Lessig, James Boyle, Cory Doctorow, and the Electronic Frontier Foundation all come to mind—to mount a powerful campaign that often overshadows other more interesting and radical approaches.[36] As a result, this aspect of the debate over 'free culture' risks being, in Ross's words, 'simply an elite copyfight between capital-owner monopolists and the labor aristocracy of the digitariat (a dominated fraction of the dominant class, as Pierre Bourdieu once described intellectuals) struggling to preserve and extend their high-skill interests'.[37]

All of this illustrates the paradox in the idea of the common Roberto Esposito locates in *Communitas*: the way in which 'the "common" is defined exactly through its most obvious antonym: what is common is that which unites the ethnic, territorial, and spiritual property of every one of its members. They have in common what is most properly their own; they are the owners of what is common to them all'.[38] What is so interesting about Esposito's philosophy when it comes to the relation between Open Education, Creative Commons and issues of copyright and intellectual property is its attempt to offer at least one way for us to begin to think community and the common in a radically different way. Esposito starts by showing that in 'all neo-Latin languages . . . "common" is what is not proper, that begins where what is proper ends'.[39] He proceeds to develop a notion of community and the common that brings into question and decentres the unified, sovereign, proprietorial subject on which Creative Commons—but also the movements for Open Access, Open Education, Free Software, and Free Culture we might add—depend:

> The common is not characterized by what is proper but by what is improper, or even more drastically, by the other; by a voiding, be it partial or whole, of property into its negative; by removing what is properly one's own that invests and decenters the proprietary subject, forcing him to take leave of himself, to alter himself. In the community, subjects do not find a principle of identification nor an aseptic enclosure within which they can establish transparent communication or even a content to be communicated. They don't find anything else except that void, that distance, that extraneousness that constitutes them as being missing from themselves.[40]

Perhaps even more interestingly in the context of some of the things we have said above in relation to free labour especially, one way of thinking about 'the central void of community', for Esposito, is in terms of the gift.[41]

NOTES

1. See http://fembotcollective.org/femtechnet/1972-2/.

2. Ian Bogost, 'MOOCs are Marketing: The Question Is, Can They Be More?', *Ian Bogost: Video Game Theory, Criticism, Design*, July 18, 2012, http://www.bogost.com/blog/moocs_are_marketing.shtml.

3. Guntram Geser, ed., *Open Educational Practices and Resources: OLCOS Roadmap 2012*, http://www.olcos.org/english/roadmap; Atkins, Brown, and Hammond, *A Review of the Open Educational Resources (OER) Movement: Achievements, Challenges, and New Opportunities*, http://www.hewlett.org/uploads/files/ReviewoftheOERMovement.pdf.

4. Andrew Ross, *Nice Work If You Can Get It: Life and Labor in Precarious Times*, 190.

5. Carole Leathwood, 'A Safe Future for Elitism', *The Guardian*, October 14, 2010, 34.

6. Mark C. Taylor, *Crisis on Campus: A Bold Plan for Reforming Our Colleges and Universities* (New York: Knopf, 2010), 163.

7. Lord Browne et al., *Securing a Sustainable Future for Higher Education: An Independent Review of Higher Education Funding and Student Finance,* October 2010, 23, https://www.gov.uk/government/uploads/system/uploads/ attachment_data/file/31999/10-1208-securing-sustainable-higher-education -browne-report.pdf.

8. Leathwood, 'A Safe Future for Elitism', 34. Taylor provides figures for the United States as follows:

> In the 1960s and 1970s, it was assumed that the public should pay for 70 to 80 percent of the cost of higher education; today many public universities receive less than 10 percent of their operating budgets from the government.
>
> These developments further increase the financial pressure on students and their families. Income has to come from somewhere. During the past twenty-five years, tuition fees have gone up 440 percent, which is four times the rate of inflation.
>
> According to a 2009 Congressional report, since 1981, the average cost of four years of college has increased 202 percent, while the consumer price index has gone up only 80 percent.
>
> Using figures from the College Board, *The Smart Student Guide to Financial Aid* concludes, "It would be reasonable to expect an average inflation rate of 7 percent or 8 percent for the next ten years'. The implications of these figures are stagger-ing. . . . In 2020 four years at a private college will cost $328,890, a decade later the price will have increased to $588,205 and by 2035 the sticker price will be $788,205. (*Crisis on Campus*, 102)

9. Department for Culture, Media and Sport, 'Making It Easier for the Me-dia and Creative Industries to Grow, While Protecting the Interests of Citizens', Gov.uk, February 27, 2013, https://www.gov.uk/government/policies/making -it-easier-for-the-media-and-creative-industries-to-grow-while-protecting -the-interests-of-citizens#Creative.

10. As Will Hutton points out, since tuition fees were raised:

> Admissions to university have held up, even if applications have fallen. . . . Yet take a closer look and the picture is more disturbing.
>
> Although the proposition was that there would be a range of fees, few universities charge less than £9,000 a year. . . . Accommodation and living costs have to be paid for on top, so that almost whatever university a student attends or whatever the degree taken, he or she will end up with about £45,000 of debt.
>
> Even so, universities such as Oxford, warned its vice-chancellor last week, may have to charge more, given that government support for teaching has been emasculated.
>
> There are insufficient jobs that pay enough to allow even a fraction of each year's 340,000 students to escape the [debt] trap. The average salary is £26,500. Only about 10% of the population earn more than £41,000. Even allowing for the fact that wages usually rise faster than prices (though they have not since 2006), it follows that many, perhaps even the majority of, students will struggle to fully pay back their debt.

86 *Chapter 6*

So far, this realisation has deterred only mature and part-time students, whose applications have fallen by 14% and 40% respectively since the benchmark year of 2010. Another pressure point is the falling applications from indebted English graduates to study for master's degrees and doctorates, especially in the humanities, and this is before the first cohort incur the full debt. Soon the only graduates carrying on their studies will be the sons and daughters of the very rich or those poorer students who can secure one of the inadequate number of bursaries, scholarships, and grants. ('Unless We Change the Way We Fund Universities, Our System Will Collapse', *The Observer*, October 13, 2013, 40, http://www.theguardian.com/commentisfree/2013/oct/13/england-leave -funding-universities-students)

11. See http://www.nchum.org/.

12. Chris Parr, 'Employers Could Use Bespoke MOOCs to Assess Candidates, Willetts Says', *Times Higher Education*, May 22, 2014, 11.

13. John Daniel, 'Making Sense of MOOCs: Musing in a Maze of Myth, Paradox and Possibility', http://academicpartnerships.com/docs/default-docu ment-library/moocs.pdf?sfvrsn=0.

14. See http://www.dsdm.org/academic.

15. A radical metrics would encourage people to work in more interesting ethical and political ways than either conventional metrics or even altmetrics: for example, by finding ways of measuring the amount of work someone shares or gives away.

16. We are aware that in-work academic labourers are paid by their institutions and many could benefit greatly from making their research and publications available on a free and open basis. However, at the same time, it is worth noting that the vast majority of (non-academic, non-affiliated) authors, artists, and musicians benefit very little from the current copyright economy. A few top stars may earn a lot, but most do not. As *The Guardian* reports on the basis of the *2014 Digital Book World and Writer's Digest Author Survey*:

54% of traditionally-published authors and almost 80% of go-it-alone writers are making less than $1,000 (£600) a year. Just over 77% of self-published writers make $1,000 or less a year . . . with a startlingly high 53.9% of traditionally-published authors, and 43.6% of hybrid authors, reporting their earnings are below the same threshold. A tiny proportion—0.7% of self-published writers, 1.3% of traditionally-published, and 5.7% of hybrid writers—reported making more than $100,000 a year from their writing. (Alison Flood, 'Figures Show the Vast Majority of Authors, Both Traditionally and Self-Published, Are Struggling to Make a Living from Their Work', *The Guardian*, January 17, 2014, http://www.theguardian.com/ books/2014/jan/17/writers-earn-less-than-600-a-year)</cite>

In *Nice Work If You Can Get It*, Andrew Ross even goes so far as to argue that:

in the court of public opinion, corporate IP warriors can always win points by broadcasting the claim that they are defending the labor rights of vulnerable artists. Yet the historical record and the experience of working artists today confirm that the struggling proprietary author has always been more of a convenient fiction for publishers to exploit than a consistent beneficiary of copyright rewards. Culture-industry executives are able to masquerade as the last line of protection for artists, when in fact they are systematically stripping them of their copyrights. (167)

If so, then it might not be just academic labourers who have much to gain from experimenting with different kinds of economies and 'alternate modernities'. This is not to say the same alternate economy which emerges in one sphere can simply be exported to other areas of society and culture. But this problem of scale is not peculiar to Open Education or even to academia: it applies to the situation of many movements and initiatives that are 'beyond the academy', too, such as those that come under the headings of Free Software, Copyleft, and CopyFarLeft. So yes, part of the medium- to longer-term task is going to be to see if we can translate the kind of 'open' experiments many of us have been involved with in our different ways into areas of society other than the academy . . . and other than those associated with what Ross calls the labour aristocracy of the digitariat as well. But that doesn't mean we shouldn't also be doing what we can where we are now. As Ngũgĩ wa Thiong'o once said in a talk he gave as part of Open Humanities Press, 'It is not enough, but it is a beginning' ('Publishing for a Global Culture', delivered at the Second International PKP Scholarly Publishing Conference, Vancouver, July 8–10, 2009).
    17. See Chantal Mouffe, *The Democratic Paradox* (London: Verso, 2000), 130; Karan Barad, *Meeting the Universe Halfway: Quantum Physics and the Entanglement of Matter and Meaning* (Durham, NC: Duke University Press, 2007). Elsewhere, Barad writes:

It is through specific agential intra-actions that the boundaries and properties of the 'components' of phenomena become determinate and that particular embodied concepts become meaningful. A specific intra-action (involving a specific material configuration of the 'apparatus of observation') enacts an *agential cut* (in contrast to the Cartesian cut—an inherent distinction—between subject and object) effecting a separation between 'subject' and 'object'. That is, the agential cut enacts a *local* resolution *within* the phenomenon of the inherent ontological indeterminacy. In other words, relata do not pre-exist relations; rather, relata-within-phenomena emerge through specific intra-actions. Crucially, the intra-actions enact *agential separability*—the local condition of *exteriority-within-phenomena*. ('Posthumanist Performativity: Toward an Understanding of How Matter Comes to Matter', *Signs: Journal of Women in Culture and Society*, vol. 28, no. 3 [2003]: 815)

18. Bogost, 'MOOCs are Marketing'.

19. This point was made separately by both Jeremy Gilbert and David Cunningham in talks given at the Visual Culture Studies Conference I (organised by New York University, University of the Arts, London, and University of Westminster, London), held at University of Westminster, May 27–29, 2010. Needless to say, it should be accompanied by a firm rejoinder that we must also fight to prevent ours from being the last such generation, and to combat the governing political and economic paradigm—neoliberal capitalism—which makes this state of affairs seem inevitable.

20. *The 1%: Strengthening Non-profits Through Design*, http://www.theone percent.org/About/Overview.htm, accessed January 26, 2014.

21. Peer Review Survey 2009, *Sense About Science: Equipping People to Make Sense of Science and Evidence*, September 8, 2009, http://www.senseabout science.org.uk/index.php/site/project/29/.

22. As Ted Striphas writes of Informa plc, the parent company of Taylor & Francis and of Routledge:

> One of Informa's subsidiaries, Adam Smith Conferences . . . specializes in organizing events designed to open the former Soviet republics to private investment. Other divisions of the company provide information, consulting, training, and strategic planning services to [major international agricultural, banking, insurance, investment, pharmaceutical, and telecommunications corporations, in addition to] government agencies. Take Robbins-Gioia, for instance. The United States Army recently tapped this Informa subsidiary during an overhaul of its command and control infrastructure. The firm was brought in to assess how well the Army had achieved its goal of 'battlefield digitization'. The United States Air Force, meanwhile, tapped Robbins-Gioia when it needed help improving its fleet management systems for U-2 spy planes. ('Acknowledged Goods: Cultural Studies and the Politics of Academic Journal Publishing', *Communication and Cultural/Critical Studies*, vol. 7, no. 1 [2010], preprint available at https://scholarworks.iu.edu/dspace/bitstream/handle/2022/6939/Differences%20%26%20Repetitions_%20_Acknowl edged%20Goods_%20Worksite.PDF?sequence=1)

23. Harvie, Lightfoot, Lilley, and Weir, 'What Are We to Do with Feral Publishers?'.

24. See Ted Bergstrom, *A Lysistratan Scheme*, 2002, http://www.econ.ucsb .edu/~tedb/Journals/lysistrata.html, accessed February 10, 2013. For more recent information about 'journal cost-effectiveness 2006–2008', see Bergstrom and Preston McAfee's website Journalprices.com, http://www.journalprices .com/.

25. Nick Montfort, 'Digital Media, Games, and Open Access', *Grand Text Auto*, December 21, 2007, http://grandtextauto.org/2007/12/21/digital-media -games-and-open-access/.

26. danah boyd, 'Open-access Is the Future: Boycott Locked-down Academic Journals', *Apophenia*, February 6, 2008, http://www.zephoria.org/thoughts/archives/2008/02/06/openaccess_is_t.html#comment-322195.

27. Harvard Faculty Advisory Council, 'Faculty Advisory Council Memorandum on Journal Pricing: Major Periodical Subscriptions Cannot Be Sustained', *The Harvard Library Transition*, April 17, 2012, http://isites.harvard.edu/icb/icb.do?keyword=k77982&tabgroupid=icb.tabgroup143448.

28. Brian Matthews, 'So I'm Editing This Journal Issue and . . . ,' *Ubiquitous Librarian*, March 23, 2013, http://chronicle.com/blognetwork/theubiquitouslibrarian/2013/03/23/so-im-editing-this-journal-issue-and/.

29. For more, see Simon Head, 'Grim Threat to British Universities', *New York Times*, January 13, 2010, http://www.nybooks.com/articles/archives/2011/jan/13/grim-threat-british-universities/?pagination=false. For the U.S. context, see Jack Schuster and Martin Finkelstein, *The American Faculty: The Restructuring of Academic Work and Careers* (Baltimore: Johns Hopkins University Press, 2006), and Sheila Slaughter and Gary Rhoades, *Academic Capitalism and the New Economy* (Baltimore: Johns Hopkins University Press, 2009).

30. Bernard Stiegler defines the difference between employment and work as follows:

> Not all employment is work: not all jobs are conducive to the acquisition and development of knowledge and therewith, to individuation, that is, the process whereby you can make a place for yourself in society as a producer, *and not only as a consumer whose job furnishes the employee with a salary which in turn confers buying power.* Individuation is on the contrary *what takes work beyond mere employment*, if ones understands that 'work' *consists in action in the world in order to transform it on the basis of knowledge one has of it.* (*La Télécratie contre la démocratie* [2006], cited in *For a New Critique of Political Economy* [London: Polity, 2010], 131, n. 12)

31. Mark Fisher, *Capitalist Realism: Is There No Alternative?* (Winchester: O Books, 1999), 79–80. It is conceivable that such a critical Open Education project could also be aligned with other movements and struggles: not just those concerned with the making precarious of graduates, including those who teach, but with those around student debt—for example, the Occupy Wall Street–inspired Rolling Jubilee Project (http://rollingjubilee.org/). That said, we would want to insist on the importance of our earlier point about the danger of closing off access to the 'political', and of the need to be wary of being complacent about immediate political needs. For more on student debt, however, see Brian Holmes, 'Silence=Debt: Life Beyond the Education Bubble', *Beyond Cognitive Capital: Another Life Just Might Be Possible*, June, 2012, http://brianholmes.files.wordpress.com/2012/06/silencedebt.pdf.

32. The P2PU's license page reads, 'Unless otherwise noted, all the materials on this site are licensed under a Creative Commons Attribution Share Alike 3.0 Unported license' ('License', available at http://p2pu.org/license, accessed April 25, 2010). A text detailing the 'lengthy and eye-opening process to reach consensus on which license would be the best to use' that members of the P2PU Community went through is available at http://docs.google.com/View?id=dc394dmc_179hdvhk33c.

For more details on intellectual property rights and Creative Commons, see Jisc's Open Educational Resources IPR support: http://www.web2rights.com/OERIPRSupport/index.html.

33. See, for example, Florian Cramer, 'The Creative Common Misunderstanding', <nettime-l> mailing list, October 9, 2006, http://www.nettime.org/Lists-Archives/nettime-l-0610/msg00025.html; republished in Florian Cramer, *Anti-media: Ephemera on Speculative Arts* (Amsterdam: Institute of Network Cultures, 2013); Dmytri Kleiner, *The Telecommumist Manifesto* (Amsterdam: Institute of Network Cultures, 2010), http://telekommunisten.net/the-telekommunist-manifesto/; and Gary Hall (forthcoming), 'Copyfight', *Critical Keywords for the Digital Humanities* (Lüneberg, Germany: Centre for Digital Culture, Leuphana University, 2014), where a version of this critique of Creative Commons was first developed.

34. Kleiner, *Telecommumist Manifesto*, 28.

35. Ross, *Nice Work If You Can Get It*, 168.

36. Ibid., 161.

37. Ibid., 169.

38. Roberto Esposito, *Communitas: The Origin and Destiny of Community* (Stanford: Stanford University Press, 2010), 3.

39. Ibid., 3.

40. Ibid., 7.

41. Ibid., 18.

7

❖ ❖

Diverse 'Disruption'

In the neo-liberal social climate of most advanced democracies today, Humanistic studies have been downgraded beyond the 'soft' sciences level, to something like a finishing school for the leisurely classes. Considered more of a personal hobby than a professional research field, I believe that the Humanities are in serious danger of disappearing from the twenty-first-century European university curriculum.

—Rosi Braidotti, *The Posthuman* (London: Polity, 2013), 10

For us, the creation of spaces for critical engagement is a necessary part of both the radical disruption of the university's more conservative and regressive practices (see chapter 1), *and* of the process of radically disrupting Open Education too, given that the latter has (intentionally or otherwise) created a new conflicted space of knowledge production. In this respect, it is important, as we say, to distinguish between different kinds of disruption. These include, but are not limited to: disruption of the practices of HEIs, not least by means of technological-pedagogic practices; disruption of the business models and economics of these institutions; and disruption of their ownership and institutional structures. For instance, many venture and multinational capital-backed Open Education start-ups are consciously aimed at disrupting the institutional structures of higher education in order to open up what to date has largely been a public institution to the penetration of their marketised solutions.

By contrast, we are interested in thinking about and exploring how so-called *digital innovations* can be created and scaled in order to produce a radical transformation in our current systems and models for the production, publication, sharing and discussion of teaching, learning and research, and with them the material practices and social relations of our own institutional labour.

Such a critically engaged approach, involving the taking of considered, responsible, political and ethical decisions, and with them the questioning of many of the ideas Open Education projects otherwise tend to take for granted, *would not* serve merely to replicate the university as it already exists, only online and in a form that is cheaper and more democratically accessible—say, by taking teaching and research created according to what is essentially a medieval model of work and delivery,[1] albeit one updated to take account of nineteenth-century mass industrialization,[2] and making it available for free online for self-learning and other non-degree-granting purposes. Quite apart from the danger of helping to produce a supposedly more flexible, efficient and cost-effective two-tier university system (along with a corresponding class of precarious university workers operating largely outside of institutional support, who, thanks to their 'stand-by-ability', can be easily employed and 'restructured' depending on the circumstances), there is too great a risk of such an online replication of the existing university merely being a way for those who already have loud voices on the net to extend their influence even further.[3] Nor would it simply mimic much twenty-first-century media in being open, fluid, collaborative and distributed in form. Yes, on occasion such an experimental, critical, pragmatic approach to Open Education might advocate moving away from the conventional, hierarchical, master/disciple, lecturer/student relation, which many new developments in digital culture are challenging just as they are challenging the relation between producer and consumer. Instead, it could provide academics, researchers, teachers and students with opportunities to share roles, knowledge and work in more open, dynamic, mobile, relational, collective, fluid and processual ways on a local, regional, national and transnational basis.[4] So as well as facilitating exchanges between students themselves, in the model of disrupted education we are proposing students could be actively involved in co-creating and developing online strategies and courses. In this way they could be encouraged to be less passively reliant on lecturers and assume more responsibility for their own teaching and learning. This might be particularly useful at a time when students are actually often more skilled at using new media technologies than many academics.

However, what is really exciting about such an experimental yet critically engaged approach to Open Education is the potential it contains for the arts and humanities, *not merely* to continue in the ('knowledge for its own sake' and public good-oriented) forms they have traditionally taken, but that are increasingly now being excluded from the university as a result of market ideology and the alignment of research funding on the part of many governments with what they perceive to be society's future industrial strengths;[5] *but also* to create spaces for the invention of new forms and new institutions for the arts and humanities. In short, the way the higher education landscape is currently being disrupted by Open Education presents us with an opportunity to radically rethink the arts and humanities themselves; and with them the very idea of the university.

MEDIA AND CULTURAL STUDIES PLC

It is perhaps no surprise that this multi-part project, engaging critically with Open Education as it does, should have emerged from a group of collaborators many of whom identify themselves with media and cultural studies. As Bill Readings showed in *The University in Ruins*, cultural studies in particular has been 'the contemporary way to speculate on the question of what it means to be *in* the University' for some time now (this role having previously belonged in the United Kingdom to English literature and elsewhere to philosophy).[6] And to be sure, for many of us involved in this project, cultural studies has on more than one occasion offered a hospitable space in which to raise the kind of difficult, awkward, troubling and, yes, disruptive questions that more traditional disciplines such as history, art history and English literature are often quite wary of. This includes questions for the following key areas:

- The institution of the university—witness the willingness of cultural studies to challenge many of the accepted material practices and social relations of university labour. E. P. Thompson's

Warwick University Ltd.: *Industry, Management and the Universities* from 1970 provides an apt example, given not just our own location (like the University of Warwick) in Coventry, but also that we too are providing a collaboratively written political philosophy with regard to the *businessification* of higher education from *within* the academy. Imagine publishing a book that engages so critically in this respect with the very university you are working for—a *Coventry University PLC*, in our case. Are the difficulties inherent in pursuing such a direct strategy today one reason Thompson's book was for so long out of print and rarely discussed, even within cultural studies (a new edition only appearing from the small, Nottingham-based left-wing press Spokesman Books in 2014)?[7]

- The more traditional disciplines within the university: via cultural studies' long history of engagement with the new, the different, the marginal, the excluded; its raising of questions around issues of power, ideology, class, race, ethnicity, gender, sexuality, the everyday and popular culture, and their relation to the social, the political, and the economic; and the adoption of a multi-, inter- and at times anti-disciplinary approach that has enabled cultural studies to draw on a wide range of literatures, epistemological traditions and methodological repertoires. According to Stuart Hall, the name 'Cultural Studies' was originally decided upon at the founding moment of the Birmingham Centre for Contemporary Cultural Studies (what is it about the West Midlands, John Henry Newman also spending his final thirty-two years in Edgbaston at the Birmingham Oratory?) with just such a purpose in mind: 'It was about as broad as we could make it; thereby we ensured that no department in either the humanities or social sciences who thought that they had already taken care of culture could fail to feel affronted by our presence. In this latter enterprise, at least, we succeeded'.[8]

Yet more than sixteen years after Readings's analysis of *The University in Ruins*, and more than forty years after the original publication of Thompson's *Warwick University Ltd*, does cultural studies continue to provide such a hospitable space for this kind of critical enquiry? Is it still the means by which the university *thinks itself*? We would like to believe so. Nevertheless, it has to be acknowledged that as the years have gone by, this difficult, awkward, troublemaking, disruptive aspect is something cultural studies, in Britain at any rate, has often attempted to marginalise or keep in check. Instead of endeavouring to remain open to new forms of politics and new ways of being political such as those that can be associated with Open Access, for example[9]— precisely the kind of openness, not just to politics but to history, too, it could be argued produced the singular work and ideas that resulted in the emergence and development of cultural studies in the first place— it seems as if cultural studies has too often resorted to the moralistic fetishisation of the politics associated with its founding thinkers, their followers and interpreters?

A number of speculative theories can be developed as to why cultural studies may have kept its tendency for disruption with certain limits:

- Out of a desire on the part of cultural studies to be, if not necessarily a 'discipline in its own right', then certainly a 'legitimate' academic field of study and research; and to be recognised, accepted and institutionalised within the university as such.[10]
- In an attempt to police and reinforce its boundaries, so as to not risk the designation 'Cultural Studies' being applied to any old collection of subjects, methods and approaches. For despite how Derrida presents it in 'The Future of the Profession or the University Without Condition', cultural studies is not what he ungenerously bundles together with interdisciplinarity as a 'good-for-everything concept'.[11] The institution of the university may in many cases want cultural studies not to be a 'project', but 'it does matter', as Stuart Hall insists, 'whether cultural studies is this or that. It can't be just any old thing which chooses to march under a particular banner. It is a serious enterprise, or project, and that is inscribed in what is sometimes called the "political" aspect of cultural studies'.[12]
- In order to maintain its identity *as a politically engaged field*. In fact, it could be argued that it is only by marginalising or delimiting what Derrida regards as the university's *right to criticise everything without condition* that cultural studies can endeavour to stabilise and maintain its (politically engaged) identity *as cultural studies*. This is why it often has to ascribe much of this

unconditionally difficult, awkward, troublemaking, disruptive aspect to disciplines such as continental philosophy or critical theory—especially when it comes to questions of politics—as this enables cultural studies to maintain its sense of being a field that is properly politically committed in a way that others are not (and this despite the fact that many other fields consider themselves to be politically committed too). From this standpoint, many of those working in cultural studies would maintain that it really does not need any more difficult troublemakers. Hence the way cultural studies has tended to distance itself from Alain Badiou's conception of politics, for example. If it discusses Badiou at all, it is too often to position his concept of the 'fidelity to an event' as being political,[13] not in the proper neo-Gramscian sense of building a strategic counter-hegemony, but only in a limited, tactical sense—which in effect means it cannot be considered particularly political at all.[14]

Does this provide an explanation as to why cultural studies has for many experienced something of a crisis over itself and politics in recent years; why it is often hard to see an engagement between 'theory' and 'politics' in much of cultural studies today?[15] Is it also why much of what goes on under the name cultural studies is 'so fucking boring', to borrow the words of Lawrence Grossberg from a few years ago?[16] Why cultural studies as a field no longer appears quite as interesting, important, and relevant as it once did? And why a lot of former devotees of cultural studies in the United Kingdom—including many of the co-authors of this study—often no longer use the term to describe what they do (preferring instead critical theory, philosophy, critical media studies, digital humanities, media arts, etc.)?

- As a result of the willingness of many academics and departments (such as indeed that in which some of us work at Coventry) to repackage or rebrand what they do as media studies for both practical and strategic reasons: because media studies is more obviously practical, vocational and instrumental, more 'business facing', more attractive to students and potential funders (and thus institutions, their managers and administrators), and easier to franchise abroad as part of the globalisation of U.K. education and so on.[17]

It is not our intention here to add to the usual stereotypical condemnations of media studies as being 'Mickey Mouse' both academically and intellectually. Media studies is obviously extremely important to us, not least with regard to our understanding of the digital media and technology that is making Open Education possible. Still there are important differences between media studies and cultural studies. And one of them is that in many of its guises, the former is often less interested in thinking what it means to be *in* the university, and of insisting on the unconditional right to criticise everything and asking the kind of difficult, awkward, disruptive questions we are referring to.[18] Is there a danger, then, of something similar happening to cultural studies in Britain as some are saying has already happened to women's studies here and elsewhere?[19] Plenty of academics may still conduct cultural studies research, but are they increasingly having to work in non-cultural studies departments in order to do so? Has this not in fact already happened to a large extent? Could we even say that this is partly a measure of the success of cultural studies in moving issues to do with culture and politics from the margins to the mainstream of academic life, and indeed society—to the point where a specific field called cultural studies is no longer seen as being needed to achieve this; that its job has been done? Or is that too optimistic a reading in the current conjuncture?

BRINGING IT ALL BACK HOME, AGAIN

It is no doubt worth emphasising that none of our insistence on proactive critical experimentation with new and emerging Open Education is intended to simply go along with the disruption to the university currently being generated by market forces (see chapter 1).[20] We strongly disagree with those who argue conventional 'universities will be irrelevant by 2020', as they will be replaced by Amazon, Google, iTunes U and TED, along with 'virtual institutions such as Western Governors University in the US'.[21] Nor is it our intention to align ourselves with the sentiment behind Bill Gates's statement at the 2010 Tech-onomy Conference: that 'place-based' universities will be far less important by just 2015.[22] What we *do* want to insist on is the need to explore the potential implications for teaching, learning and research, and for the material practices and social relations of our own institutional labour, of new forms of networked technologies, open access digital publishing, collaborative web tools and sociable spaces to enhance educational activity, so as not to let the future of the university—and with it the organisation of post-industrial society and the constitution of knowledge—be dominated by the likes of Microsoft, Apple and Tim O'Reilly; or Khan Academy, Udacity, Coursera, or FutureLearn, for that matter.[23]

Yet we would go even further than this. We would actually be suspicious of an emphasis on the future of this kind: for the simple reason it distracts us from the fact that many of the changes we are discussing—in terms of new ways of organising education and rethinking our relation to knowledge, what it is and how it is generated, communicated and shared—can be made right now. The main reason these changes have not already been made is due to *political decisions*, not because all this occupies the realm of futurology.

To end by providing one modest example of what is possible, *right here, right now*, in the Media Department at Coventry School of Art and Design, we have launched four Open Media courses in the last few years, designed to make freely accessible a series of high-quality teaching and learning experiences and related resources, and also provide access to networks and communities of subject specialists, professional practitioners, mentors and wider learning communities.[24] These classes have been developed by staff, students and visiting contributors to the department. But they also invite live online participation and contribution from other HEIs, professional practice networks and communities of media researchers, teachers and learners *synchronously* with their face-to-face delivery at Coventry (rather than post-hoc or a-synchronously, as in the case of MIT's OpenCourseWare, say).

Our experience is that students in the Media Department at Coventry benefit enormously from this manner of 'Open' working—which is partly how we justify it to the university. For example, students gain access to a vastly expanded range of resources; they have been given feedback and commentary by scholars and practitioners from all over the world; while the exposure of, and commentary on, their practical work has led to opportunities for projects, placements, and opportunities at levels beyond any previously available.

However, and importantly, it is not just students at Coventry who benefit: in our own particular *hybrid* take on 'blended learning' classes on these courses are open online to anyone, anywhere, to participate in, add to the discussions and even rip, remix and mash-up. This applies to the schedule, lectures, lesson contents, exercises and assignments, recommended reading, recorded talks and interviews with visiting speakers (audio and video), RSS feeds, tag clouds and blog post archive, as well as a number of practical 'how-to' videos, all of which are available under a CC-BY-SA license. The use of blogs, Vimeo, Flickr, Twitter and other social media platforms means that participants—both the in-class ('atoms based'), accredited, fee-paying participants and those taking these open classes for free remotely—can interact and contribute through discussion, feedback, suggestions, etc. In this way the syllabus thus becomes a 'co-authored script', curated by the academic team 'but produced by the collective exchange and effort of the learning community'.[25]

Picturing the Body (Picbod) and Photography and Narrative (Phonar), which are led by Jonathan Worth with the assistance of Matt Johnston, are the two longest standing of these open courses, the first dating from 2009 (long before the launch of xMOOCs such as Udacity and Coursera in 2012).[26] These ten-week undergraduate classes enable academics, researchers, students and practitioners from both inside and outside the university to collaboratively produce, curate and engage with a wide range of media and educational resources relating to photography. The most recent of these courses is an undergraduate class focused on creative activism, which was launched between January and March 2012, and led this time by Pete Woodbridge.[27] Again, the class and its materials are made freely available online on an open basis to enable anyone worldwide to participate in the class, join in the discussions or even rip and remix the content. Those interested can also download the content and participate in the ongoing class discussion through iTunes U and the Peer 2 Peer University, it being important to us on both a 'philosophical and practical level that the online elements of the classes live within the existing networked ecology of the Web, using free and open access tools and platforms'.[28] The class itself explores the potential of creative media activism by encouraging the participants to experiment with creating live interventions as well as getting involved in a number of crucial cultural, political and social debates. Over the ten-week course it looks at how media activists, creatives and campaigners have used their media knowledge, connections and skills to ask questions, provoke debate and raise awareness of important issues in their local, national and international communities.

But all this is just one experiment with Open Education. We need others—there need to be lots of them as our own work is far from being an answer in itself. Indeed, far from this period of financial crisis, when so many jobs, institutions and courses appear to be at risk, being an unpromising moment to be thinking about exploring new ways of organising education and rethinking our relation to knowledge, we would argue that this is precisely the moment we should be doing so. Moments of crisis can also be moments of opportunity, provided we summon 'the courage to defend and practice our ideas and principles, to say what we think, what we want', to quote Alain Badiou.[29] And this is as true for the university, as it moves from the industrial factory model of the eighteenth, nineteenth, and twentieth centuries to some as yet-to-be-established twenty-first-century post-industrial form, as it is for society.

NOTES

1. 'Lectures and seminars offered in today's colleges and universities are still similar in style and format to those delivered in classrooms in the 1700s, with professors—and, increasingly adjuncts and graduate students—lecturing to hundreds of students who passively transcribe the spoken word like medieval scribes recording the holy writ' (Taylor, *Crisis on Campus*, 14).

2. By updating to account for nineteenth-century mass industrialisation we are referring to individual experts 'broadcasting' (that is, to a large audience on a one-to-many basis) an education suitable for mass consumption in that it is divided into separate faculties and departments. Each has its own distinct area of expertise and competence, and each is packaged as individual course units, all of which conform (in terms of their length, level, size, and so forth) to a set of standards and values certified centrally. However, for the classic account of the division of the university into faculties, see Immanuel Kant, *The Conflict of the Faculties* (New York: Abaris, 1979).

3. As Michael Gurstein writes:

> The issue with networks of course is that they are presumably open to all. So one must ask—say in the case of the twenty-first-century university as Global Learning Networks—will these networks function as the university equivalent of the They-

WorkForYou.com network where it was quite clear I think, that the already influential were using their enhanced capability for information access and digital networking to, in fact, extend their reach and make their 'louder voices' even louder. Content certainly won't come from the 70% of the world's population who don't have access to the Internet, the main instrumentality of the emerging global learning network.

And they won't come from the roughly 50% of the US (and much large proportion of the world's) population that lacks the functional literacy skills to access and use a simple data intensive (e-government) website. They are even less likely to come from the 90% of the African population who can't afford Internet access even if the rates they were expected to pay were at world levels rather than at artificially high and exploitative levels.

So my question is, in the context of this emerging 'Twenty-first Century University as global learning network(s)'—whose will be the 'louder' voices providing the content and context in these networks; what content will they be providing; how relevant will it be to the needs of the excluded and the marginalized; and overall what measures might be in place to ensure that the softer and weaker voices—those representing the urban and rural poor, indigenous people in both Developed but particularly in Developing Countries; the landless and the migrants—are in fact heard and responded to and even given value, legitimacy and resonance within these networks. ('Louder Voices and Learning Networks', *Gurstein's Community Informatics*, June 25, 2011, http://gurstein.wordpress.com/2011/06/25/louder-voices-and-learning-networks/)

4. David Campbell writes:

Opening up in the link economy also means altering the ethos of teaching, moving it away from the broadcast structure of the lecture to new modes of student engagement. Professors will cease to be people who 'profess' and become people who curate flows of information, establishing the conditions of possibility for critical collaboration.

The new ecology of the web and its impact on the structure of information requires a fundamental rethink of pedagogy. However, this rethink does not mean that education inevitably migrates on-line. Students are often initially against change because they feel it is a step towards a virtual process with no personal contact. What is needed, as [Michael] Wesch argues, are ways to leverage the social media environment for a pedagogical process that is open, collaborative, linked, distributed, and above all else, engaging. ('Revolutions in the Media Economy (4)—Disturbing the University', *David Campbell*, October 1, 2009, http://www.david-campbell.org/2009/10/01/revolutions-in-the-media-economy-4/)

5. For more, see Jonathan Bate, ed. *The Public Value of the Humanities* (London, Bloomsbury, 2011); John Holmwood, ed. *A Manifesto for the Public University* (London: Bloomsbury, 2011); and Thomas Docherty, *For the University: Democracy and the Future of the Institution* (London: Bloomsbury, 2013).

6. Bill Readings, *The University in Ruins* (Cambridge, MA, and London: Harvard University Press, 1996), 118.

7. E. P. Thompson, ed., *Warwick University Ltd: Industry, Management and the Universities* (Nottingham: Spokesman, 2014). At the time of writing, Thomas Docherty, a professor of English and comparative literature at Warwick and member of the steering group of the Council for the Defence of British Universities, has been suspended from the university, and prevented from speaking at a June 2014 conference there on Warwick University Ltd: Lessons from 1970 and the Higher Education Sector Today, allegedly for his criticisms of higher education policy in the United Kingdom and the marketisation and bureaucratisation of universities.

8. Stuart Hall, 'Race, Culture and Communications: Looking Backward and Forward at Cultural Studies', in Marcus E. Green, ed., *Rethinking Gramsci* (Oxon: Routledge, 2011), 11. We should note that in some parts of academia this has subsequently been received as a rather colonizing gesture on the part of cultural studies. Especially at the height of its institutional success in the United States, Australia, and elsewhere during the 1980s and 1990s, it was seen as having led to the marginalisation of other disciplines, including philosophy and literature, on the grounds such subjects could be dealt with better and more interestingly from within cultural studies. This is one reason sometimes given to explain the rise in influence among a younger generation of scholars of Alain Badiou, and in particular his championing of a rather disciplinary form of philosophy (compared to the more interdisciplinary approach of previously dominant French thinkers such as Deleuze, Derrida, and Foucault).

9. See Clare Birchall and Gary Hall, 'Cultural Studies and Theory: Once More from the Top With Feeling', in Paul Smith, ed. *The Renewal of Cultural Studies* (Philadelphia: Temple University Press, 2011).

10. Stuart Hall, 'Cultural Composition: Stuart Hall on Ethnicity and the Discursive Turn', *Journal of Composition Theory*, vol. 18, no. 2 (1998): 191.

11. Jacques Derrida, 'The Future of the Profession or the University Without Condition (Thanks to the "Humanities" *What Could Take Place* Tomorrow)', in Tom Cohen, ed. *Jacques Derrida and the Humanities: A Critical Reader* (Cambridge: Cambridge University Press, 2001), 50.

12. Stuart Hall, 'Cultural Studies and Its Theoretical Legacies', in Lawrence Grossberg, Cary Nelson, and Paula Treichler, eds. *Cultural Studies* (New York: Routledge, 1992), 278.

13. Alain Badiou, *Saint Paul: The Foundation of Universalism* (Stanford: Stanford University Press, 2003), 42.

14. See, for example, Jeremy Gilbert, *Anti-capitalism and Culture: Radical Theory and Popular Politics* (Oxford: Berg, 2008), 213–16.

15. For one of many possible examples, see Nick Couldry, 'The Project of Cultural Studies: Heretical Doubts, New Horizons', in Paul Smith, ed. *The Renewal of Cultural Studies.* However, this is a common complaint that was

already being made several years earlier—for instance, by many participants at the Cultural Studies Now conference held at the University of East London, July 19–22, 2007.

16. Lawrence Grossberg, 'Does Cultural Studies Have Futures? Should It? (Or What's the Matter with New York?)', *Cultural Studies*, vol. 20, no. 1 (January 2006): 8.

17. In an article explaining why her university, Westminster, was the 'first to offer a degree in media studies', and is 'going to be the first to chuck it out', Sally Feldman noted that 'between 1997 and 2006, the number of media studies undergraduates rose by 344 per cent' ('Taking the Mickey Out', *Times Higher Education*, January 24, 2008, 27).

18. In this respect, much of what John Durham Peters has ascribed to cultural studies at its 'worst' we would be tempted to ascribe to media studies—were it not for our reluctance to indulge in anything so lacking in the kind of intellectual generosity and hospitality we have learned from cultural studies. We would certainly not be inclined to do so without actually naming and endeavouring to produce a rigorous reading of some of the texts and thinking we are referring to. This is why, as we said, we do not want to join in with the usual stereotypical condemnations of media studies. Unfortunately, Peters does not appear to suffer from such qualms as far as cultural studies is concerned. Peters writes:

> It is a commonplace that one utility of the worst form of cultural studies is the provision to young scholars of a swift mode of article production: take theory, find object, write article. The stunning global success of cultural studies in university curriculums over the past decade might be read as an academic parallel to neo-liberal economic policies. Cultural studies allows for just-in-time production, has low start-up costs and low barriers to entry in terms of knowledge, is closely allied with the act of media consumption, and supplies the increasingly important cultural industries with savvy employees. Multinational corporations are leading the charge for knowledge of local culture and languages as essential for global salesmanship. Cultural studies is a ready brand for academic entrepreneurs to market, and many countries seem to have one or two professors who act as its franchise owners. It is clear that universities are under global and regional pressure to standardize and that cultural studies meets a pragmatic need. Cultural studies has what Innis called a space bias: it travels light, favors soldiers and merchants over sages and priests, and tends to favor the contemporary over deep time. ('Strange Sympathies: Horizons of Media Theory in America and Germany', *Electronic Book Review*, June 4, 2009, http://www.electronicbookreview.com/thread/criticalecologies/myopic)

19. See, for example, Wendy Brown, 'The Impossibility of Women's Studies', *Edgework: Critical Essays on Knowledge and Politics* (Princeton and Oxford: Princeton University Press, 2005).

20. See, for example, Clayton M. Christensen and Henry J. Eyring, *The Innovative University: Changing the DNA of Higher Education From Inside Out* (London: John Wiley and Sons, 2011).

21. See Elaine Jarvik, 'Universities will be "Irrelevant" by 2020, Y. Professor says', *Deseret News*, April 30, 2009, http://www.deseretnews.com/article/705298649/Universities-will-be-irrelevant-by-2020-Y-professor-says.html.

22. 'Five years from now on the Web for free you'll be able to find the best lectures in the world. It will be better than any single university. . . . After all, what are we trying to do? We're trying to take education that today the tuition is, say, $50,000 a year so over four years—a $200,000 education—that is increasingly hard to get because there's less money for it because it's not there, and we're trying to provide it to every kid who wants it. . . . And only technology can bring that down, not just to $20,000 but to $2,000. So yes, place-based activity in that college thing will be five times less important than it is today'. (Bill Gates, cited by Jeff Young, 'Bill Gates Predicts Technology Will Make "Place-Based" Colleges Less Important in 5 Years', *Chronicle of Higher Education*, August 9, 2010, http://chronicle.com/blogPost/Bill-Gates-Predicts-Technology/26092/)
Gates's talk is available at https://www.youtube.com/watch?v=p2Qg80MVvYs.

23. See Dan Colman, 'Tim O'Reilly: The University as an Open iPhone Platform', *Open Culture*, March 24, 2010, http://www.openculture.com/. O'Reilly's talk is available at http://vimeo.com/9501220.

24. See http://openmediaclasses.covmedia.co.uk/.

25. Jonathan Shaw, *NewFotoScapes* (Birmingham: Library of Birmingham, 2014), 11, http://newfotoscapes.org/home.

26. See http://www.picbod.covmedia.co.uk and http://phonar.covmedia.co.uk. For more on these open classes, see Howard Rheingold's interview with Coventry's Jonathan Shaw, 'Global Transmedia MOOCs', *Dmlcentral*, August 30, 2012, http://dmlcentral.net/blog/howard-rheingold/global-transmedia-moocs.

27. See http://www.creativeactivism.net.

28. Shaw, *NewFotoScapes*, 10.

29. Alain Badiou, *The Communist Hypothesis* (London and New York: Verso, 2010), 66.

Index

About the Authors

Open Education: A Study in Disruption is co-authored by Coventry University's Open Media Group and Mute Publishing, as a critical experiment with both collaborative, processual writing and concise, medium-length forms of shared attention.

Pauline van Mourik Broekman, Co-founder, Mute, and Mute collective member.

Gary Hall is Director of the Centre for Disruptive Media at Coventry University, UK, and visiting professor at the Hybrid Publishing Lab—Leuphana Inkubator, Leuphana University, Germany. He is also co-founder (in 1999) of the open access journal Culture Machine, a pioneer of OA in the humanities, and co-founder (in 2006) of Open Humanities Press, which was the first open access publisher explicitly dedicated to critical and cultural theory. He is the author and editor of several books on digital culture and the idea of the university, the best known of which is *Digitize This Book!: The Politics of New Media, or Why We Need Open Access Now* (2008).

Ted Byfield is a New York–based independent researcher and writer. He served for over a decade on the design faculty of the New School University, and is a former visiting fellow at Yale Law School's Information Society Project. He co-founded the Open Syllabus Project research network, and since 1998 has co-moderated the <nettime> mailing list.

Shaun Hides is Head of Department of Media and Co-director of the Disruptive Media Learning Lab, Coventry University, UK. He authored the Department's Open Media strategy, led a JISC-funded OER project on open-connected teaching innovation and has spoken at numerous events on OER, Innovation and the impact of disruptive technologies on education. He is an advisor to the British Council.

Simon Worthington is a Research Associate at the Hybrid Publishing Consortium—Leuphana Inkubator, Leuphana University, Germany.

Original idea and direction:

Jonathan Shaw is Co-director of the Disruptive Media Learning Lab, Coventry University, UK, visiting fellow at the Centre for Excellence in Media Practice at Bournemouth University and the Chair of the Associate for Photography in Higher Education. He was awarded a Direct Fellowship of Royal Photographic Society (RPS), and a Fellowship of the Royal Society for the encouragement of Arts, Manufactures and Commerce (RSA), in recognition for his achievements in Photography and innovative educational practices.